THE
CONSULTING
PROCESS
IN
ACTION

Second Edition

THE CONSULTING PROCESS IN ACTION

SECOND EDITION

Gordon Lippitt
Ronald Lippitt

University Associates, Inc.
8517 Production Avenue
San Diego, California 92121

Copyright © 1986 by University Associates, Inc.
ISBN: 0-88390-201-X
Library of Congress Catalog Card Number: 86-19693

Printed in the United States of America

Library of Congress Cataloging-in-Publication Data

Lippitt, Gordon L.
    The consulting process in action.

    Bibliography: p.
    1. Business consultants.   I. Lippitt, Ronald.
II. Title.
HD69.C6L54   1986   658.4'6   86-19693
ISBN 0-88390-201-X

Senior Editor: Carol Nolde

Cover Designer
    & Production Artist: Ann Beaulieu

⇔ Dedication ⇔

*To Gordon, co-author, separated from collaboration by death in
December 1985. Our teamwork continued and the product you
have here is completely ours, even when I held the pen for him.*

Ronald Lippitt

Preface

During the past thirty-five years, we have worked at providing help to individuals and groups from all walks of life. One great reward and challenge of helping people is the opportunity to be a learner all the time. The act of helping is always a collaborative, problem-solving process in which the helper has as much chance to learn as those who are helped.

During the past ten years, our special challenge has been to know how to share with others what we have learned about consulting. Each of us has organized and published some of his learnings, but in this volume we have shared our learnings with each other. We have organized them in compact form in an effort to contribute to the growing needs of professional and nonprofessional helpers: consultants, counselors, supervisors, administrators, friends, advisors, and many others.

The most general term for this helping process is *consultation*. The function of consultants is *part* of the role and function of all those who lead, direct, teach, or interact as friends and peers with others. To simplify our communication, we have addressed all of you as consultants in this volume, although we recognize that consultation may be only one aspect of the jobs of many of you who also administer, direct, supervise, minister, treat, and so forth.

At various points we have distinguished between the *internal* consultant, who is located in the same setting, organization, or institution that he or she is serving, and the *external* consultant, who offers his or her help as an outsider. Often this distinction is important in determining the type of help that is feasible, appropriate, or credible.

Some of you have had training in consultation as part of your professional education; others have learned primarily on the job. Judging by our own professional education and experience, we are confident that all of us know only a little of what there is to learn about being an effective and versatile helper. Nevertheless, we believe that in this volume you will find concepts, strategies, and techniques that will be valuable additions to your repertoire.

In offering you our reflections, experiences, and learnings about consultation, we are mindful of our indebtedness to and support from:

- Our graduate students;
- The many participants in our workshops on consultation;
- Our colleagues, co-consultants, and co-trainers; and
- Our families, with whom many of the most important confrontations of our concepts and skills have been worked through.

In this revision of our first volume, we have deleted very little; but we have added a great deal of material that we believe greatly strengthens our first effort. We have supplemented our analyses of interventions; enhanced the chapter on ethical dilemmas and value guidelines; expanded the action-research model to include data from intuition; and added new chapters on designing participative learning, examples of consultation in action, guidelines for international consulting, the consultant as change facilitator, and implications for the future of consulting.

The process of consultation is challenging, awesome, rewarding, and humbling. It is not a science; but as a performing art, it requires the constant growth of those who practice it. We welcome you to some of our growth experiences and learnings.

Gordon Lippitt
Ronald Lippitt

Contents

1

Consultation: An Expanding Process

Consultation is a two-way interaction—a process of seeking, giving, and receiving help. Consulting is aimed at aiding a person, group, organization, or larger system in mobilizing internal and external resources to deal with problem confrontations and change efforts.

The values, intentions, and behaviors of consultative interaction differ from those of leadership, supervision, evaluation, therapy, and friendship. However, many people function in a consultative way when carrying out some of the tasks involved in their primary roles as administrators, supervisors, counselors, therapists, friends, or parents.

The role of a growing number of people in our society is labeled *consultant* to describe their helping functions. Many of these consultants are designated as *external* because they function as helpers from the outside of a system. Others perform as *internal* consultants, operating as part of the systems they are attempting to help.

HELPERS: PROFESSIONAL AND VOLUNTEER

Throughout history there have been individuals who acquired or were given status and credibility in groups as helpers in solving problems. Tribal wise men, medicine men and women, and priests often developed special skills as helpers in personal or group problem solving. Although preparation for the helping role did not involve any professional training program, there were apprenticeships and selection for talent. Later, charismatic leaders, such as Buddha, Christ, Muhammad, and Confucius developed circles of followers who, through role modeling, conceptual

1

training, and some supervised practice, developed helping orientations and skills and presented themselves to people as helpers and change agents.

Formal training programs and internships developed as preparation and certification, first for religious ministries and for medical practice, then for psychologists, social workers, and public health workers. Helping tended to be differentiated into consulting and training.

In recent years, individuals have been professionally trained to help solve the problems of all functions of the modern community: business management, labor leadership, education, health, public service, social welfare, recreation, religion, corrections and rehabilitation, and personal therapy.

There has also been a resurgence of the amateur or lay helper. The volunteer helper plays a critical role as his or her "brother's keeper," good neighbor, or citizen volunteer. Perhaps the most exciting development is the general recognition that it is desirable and appropriate to participate in workshops and other programs for learning the skills of helping. Courses in helping or consultation skills are offered in many university programs and by such organizations as University Associates and National Training Laboratories (NTL) Institute for Applied Behavioral Science.

THE GROWING NEED

Several futurists have pointed out that one outcome of the increasing rate of change is the increasing complexity of the problems to be solved and, consequently, the need for integration of different disciplines or sources of expertise or experience. Several trends appear to be related to this need for increased mobilization of problem-solving intelligence, and these trends present implications for the growth and development of consultation resources.

1. *Technological Development.* The rapid rate of technological development is a pervasive trend that has had and will continue to have an impact on life styles; social organization of enterprises; and the political and economic systems of the community, state, and nation. Increasingly complex problems of interdependence, welfare, education, leadership,

and decision making are being created. There is a much greater need for individuals and groups to collaborate, to ask for and to give help, and to support one another. But the motivations and skills of people lag far behind the increased need and the increased knowledge of how to solve problems, how to generate and use resources, and how to set up collaborative efforts.

2. *Crisis in Human Resources.* People are more and more conscious of the underutilization, underdevelopment, and misuse of such resources as racial and ethnic minority groups, women, children and youth, the handicapped, the elderly, the unemployed, and the undereducated. This misuse represents a great challenge to both professional and volunteer helpers.

3. *Undeveloped Consulting Skills of Workers.* It has been discovered that many managerial and nonmanagerial workers have undeveloped skills as consultants, coaches, teachers, trainers, and counselors. These people are being identified, recruited, and trained to function part-time as members of their organizations' training networks, pools of group facilitators, and internal consultants. These innovations have increased the pool of helping talent.

4. *Discretionary Time.* More and more people have discretionary time to spend beyond the demands of wage-earning and life-maintenance activities. This time is available for creative volunteer work. The quality of community life and individual lives could be improved if interpersonal helping and support could become a valued and skilled activity. "Good neighboring" could become a rewarding priority and a revitalization of democracy.

A consequence of these four trends is the fact that the needs for help are accelerating faster than the preparation of professional helpers—consultants, trainers, and teachers. This means that the need for part-time helpers, paraprofessional aides, and volunteers will continue to increase rapidly. Top priority should be given to the recruiting and training of these nonprofessionals in the skills of helping and supporting and to the creating of teams of professionals and volunteers as helping-consulting teams.

INADEQUATE RESPONSE
TO THE GROWING NEED

Several factors greatly inhibit the development of skilled and motivated consultants and leaders of helping teams: the territorial attitudes of university departments, the specializations of disciplines, and the lack of curriculum collaboration between the departments and the professional schools. The professional schools tend to lack the concepts and practices of participatory learning, placing emphasis on traditional lecture procedures and case material rather on than supervised practice to assure skill development. The spread of participatory management, although slow, is more rapid than the spread of participatory learning in higher education.

Because of their orientation, those who need help also contribute to the lack of effective consultation. A typical crisis orientation usually means that serious pain must by felt before there is motivation to seek help, and then the time pressures for rapid solution make effective consultation very difficult.

Another serious and pervasive block are the notions that "doing it oneself" is the greatest sign of competence and that asking for help is a sign of weakness. Because the highest value in an organization is usually placed on the line people who are the producers, typically there is reluctance to invest in staff people, such as internal consultants. If help is needed, organizations tend to depend on inside resources in order to "keep it in the family." Often the specific type of help needed to work on particular problems is not available within the organization, but either people are reluctant to seek the appropriate outside help or they lack the knowledge of how to do so.

To summarize, the potential users of consulting services are uninformed about identifying, recruiting, and utilizing consultation resources. They tend to reject diagnosis as a necessary starting point for working toward the solution of a particular problem. They lack perspective on necessary budget requirements; they are oriented toward seeking someone to provide ready-made answers rather than toward using methodological help in problem solving.

In addition, those who provide help lack training in interdisciplinary teamwork as internal or external problem solvers. They also lack the training to be "system thinkers."

The foregoing discussion is only a small sample of the reasons why the use of consultation resources lags so far behind the need and why the professionals and volunteers who are attempting to fill consultant roles are relatively unprepared to do flexible, competent jobs in different problem-solving situations.

DIMENSIONS OF THE HELPING PROCESS

The following paragraphs present a framework for some of the dimensions we use in discussing the process of helping. Later chapters fill in this framework.

Phases of Consultation

It is useful to think of the consultation process in terms of six phases. These phases and the types of helping work that both the client and the consultant must do in each phase are examined in Chapter 2.

Consultation Roles or Functions

The functional differences and similarities between internal and external consultants and between professional and volunteer helpers are delineated in Chapter 4, along with the ways in which these differences of position and responsibility affect the kind of help each can give. A dozen different role functions are identified in this chapter, so that a consultant can clarify his or her role and function at any point in the process of giving help. Every competent helper must be flexible enough to function in a variety of roles.

Intervention Contexts

As the reader will discover in this volume, we approach the challenge of helping the client with the proactive posture of exploring readiness and potential for improvement rather than the reactive posture of focusing on the diagnosis of pain. It will become clear that this does not mean avoiding dealing with the pain and problem but rather converting the situation, for the client, into gaining perspective on preferred outcomes of the problem-pain context.

Consultants can become involved in a wide variety of problem contexts. The strategies of giving help tend to be different in these different contexts, and we explore these contexts and their accompanying strategies in Chapter 3. The following is a brief identification of some of the intervention contexts:

- The *downsizing* situation, in which the client needs help with the challenges and requirements of cutback (doing more with less);
- The *expansion, rapid-growth* situation, in which the client is facing the complexities and heady challenges of expansion of enterprise;
- The *decentralization* situation, in which major shifts are occurring in the client's accountability and communication structure;
- The *merger* situation, in which two or more systems are facing the challenges and requirements of combining structures and functions;
- The *quality-improvement* situation, in which a decision has been made to focus on the improvement of the quality of the product and the production process;
- The *demonstration-and-dissemination* situation, in which an innovation or a new personnel practice is being tried in one part of the system, with the intention of disseminating the learnings and model to all relevant parts of the system; and
- The *entropy-prevention* situation, in which the focus is on preventing the loss of momentum and maintaining the charge that develops in most major change efforts.

One of the challenges of mature consultation is to develop a diagnostic sensitivity to these context differences and a repertoire of appropriately different strategies.

Types of Client Systems

In some cases the client system is either a person or a small, interpersonal unit, such as a couple or a family; in others the client may be a small group (for example, a team, a committee, or a staff unit). The client also may be a total organizational system (for example, a company, an agency, a bureau, or an association); or it may be an interorganizational system, such as a community, a state or nation, or an international system. The size of the client system influences decisions concerning the credibility and competencies required of the consultant and the type and size of consultation design.

Some consultants tend to specialize and work with certain types of client systems. Other consultants are generalists with respect to types of client systems, but specialize in terms of the kinds of problems they help with and the methods they use.

Clients can be classified according to their type of functions, operations, and products. Examples are as follows:

- Economic systems: business, industry, chambers of commerce, associations;
- Political systems: political parties, city governments, League of Women Voters, governors' offices;
- Educational systems: schools, colleges, adult-education programs, state departments of education;
- Religious systems: churches, seminaries, monasteries;
- Recreational and leisure-time systems: recreation programs, agencies, parks, camps, hobby clubs;
- Cultural-enrichment systems: theaters, museums, art schools, musical societies;
- Welfare systems: poverty programs, unemployment programs, food programs, subsidized housing;
- Health systems: hospitals, clinics, health-education programs;
- Social-protection agencies: courts, police, legal aid, civil liberties;
- Mass-communication systems: newspapers, radio, television; and
- Geographic entities: neighborhoods, communities, counties, regions.

All of these systems currently have programs for recruiting, training, and using professional and volunteer helpers; but the needs are greater than the resources. The opportunities for professional consultants and trained volunteer helpers are growing in all of these parts of community and national life.

Contracts and Focuses

A helping relationship may vary greatly in duration and sequence; for example, it may be:

- A one-contract relationship, a single consultation, a one-day institute, or a brief workshop;
- A single major contract with a sequence of follow-up supportive relationships;
- A defined series of sessions (six weekly sessions, a semester course, a three-phase training program); or
- An indeterminant helping contract, with termination to be mutually determined when the work is done.

The relationship may be informally defined, or a formal consulting contract may be developed.

The consultant must appropriately focus his or her helping effort to promote the problem-solving work that is needed. The focus may be on any of the following areas:

- The functioning of a total system (the whole family, the staff group, the total agency);
- One part of the client system (the mother, the company president, one department);
- One function or problem of the client (setting goals, removing stereotypes, improving trust, making decisions more efficiently); or
- The relationship between or among two or more persons, groups, or interagency relationships.

A helping intervention can also be focused in terms of the type of work to be done. For example, the efforts of the consultant may be focused on certain kinds of task work or process work. Task work may include mobilizing resources, setting goals, clarifying values, projecting alternatives, developing evaluation plans, and the many other focuses mentioned in Chapter 2. Process work may focus on mediating conflicts, developing trust, uncovering hidden agendas, and identifying blockages in communication.

The Expanding Role of Professional Helper

We have found it difficult to define in any clear-cut way the boundaries of the role of consultant or professional helper. The role keeps expanding and the learning challenges extending. The following are a few ways in which we have been able to expand the role for ourselves:

1. ***Develop the Skills of Co-Consultants.*** The increasing complexity of clients' problems and the learning and support potential of teamwork have led us to place a very high value on forming a team with one or two colleagues in consulting activities. This means paying attention to our working relations and finding ways to improve team effectiveness as we work with clients. The quality of our performance increases as we focus on planning for our clients, on complementary roles in consulting, and on debriefing thoroughly to learn from each experience and to plan improvement.

2. ***Incorporate Client Representatives into the Consulting Team.*** With every client we attempt to include at least one or two people from within the client system as part of the co-consulting team. It is usually quite easy to obtain top-management approval of this idea because a major rationale is that we will contribute to the skills of the inside team members and make it possible for them to take over all or most of our functions. One great advantage for us is that insiders provide diagnostic sensitivity, feedback about client reactions, and access to the key network of internal personnel.

3. ***Develop Facilitators Within the Client System.*** To ensure the quality and continuity of our consulting interventions, we find that it is crucial to develop process facilitators in all parts of the client system. In every work unit, there are individuals who are curious and sensitive about "making things work better." With the support of their supervisors, we recruit and train them as meeting facilitators, quality coaches, task-force conveners, and training-network members. In one client system, for example, one hundred and fifty line members of the training network have completely changed the depth and quality of the training program; they give ten to fifteen days a year to this management-supported function.

4. ***Enhance the Flexibility and Variety of the Consulting Repertoire.*** We used to have clear boundaries separating the functions of consultant, trainer, counselor, and information specialist. With our years of practice, however, these boundaries have faded; as the problem-solving work with the client requires, we function in any or all of these ways. The subject of building a repertoire is explained in Chapter 3.

5. ***Offer Opportunities to Young Professionals Who Want to Grow.*** We feel that providing hands-on learning opportunities on an apprentice or intern basis is a crucial complement to the concept-focused learning activities of most professional and discipline-training programs.

CONCLUSION

In the subsequent chapters, we have attempted to explain the basic orientation to helping that has emerged for us during our years of practice. Our intention is to pass on some of the concepts, designs, and tools that have become essential aspects of our intervention repertoire as professional helpers.

2

Phases in Consulting

Each step in the process of consulting confronts the helper and the client with a series of interaction decisions and possible alternatives for behavioral strategy. These interaction decisions and behaviors may be the responses of a would-be helper to the expressions of need, concern, or pain of a client (person or group); or they may be initiated by the helper to stimulate a desire for help, to establish a helping contract, and to activate problem-solving efforts on the part of the client.

These interactions may be part of the informal process of give-and-take between peers; examples include the voluntary efforts of friends and the more deliberative efforts of parents or more experienced people to help with problems. On the other hand, such interactions may be the efforts of professional helpers—doctors, lawyers, social workers, psychologists, organization development (OD) specialists—to provide services as set out in formal contracts. A helper may be *internal* to the client group or system (for example, an internal consultant, a member of the same family, or a supervisor in the same department) or *external,* offering the more removed perspective of an outsider.

In our experience the phases of the consulting process are equally applicable to all types of helping relationships, although the roles that are assumed and the intervention decisions that are made differ significantly. We have identified six major phases in any consultant-client working relationship:

1. Engaging in initial contact and entry;
2. Formulating a contract and establishing a helping relationship;
3. Identifying problems through diagnostic analysis;
4. Setting goals and planning for action;
5. Taking action and cycling feedback; and
6. Completing the contract (continuity, support, and termination).

11

The following is a brief review of the types of working tasks (work focuses) that are involved in each of these phases. Included as part of the discussion of each work focus are excerpts from our taped dialogs in which we share illustrative case situations from our consulting experiences.

PHASE I: ENGAGING IN INITIAL CONTACT AND ENTRY

Work Focus 1: Making First Contact

The initial contact with regard to a potential consulting relationship may come from any of the following three sources:

1. *The Potential Client.* A sense of pain or a problem may be interpreted as a need to seek help, accompanied by an awareness that certain kinds of consultation may be appropriate sources of help. Or there may be no pain, but instead a desire to increase one's competitive advantage by improving productivity and effectiveness or to improve satisfaction with one's self-image. An organization's normal operating procedure, for example, may be to seek out and use consultants. Contacting a particular consultant or consulting group may be a result of previous experience, awareness of the consultant's reputation, knowledge of the consultant's specialization in particular problems, or merely a shopping expedition to find out what is available.

2. *The Potential Consultant.* Contact may be motivated by a general search for new clients or the consultant's knowledge that he or she has been helpful to other, similar client systems. The consultant may perceive a pattern of functional ineffectiveness similar to that which he or she has coped with before. Contact may be initiated because the consultant has particular priorities, such as helping any group trying to improve the quality of its environment or developing participation in decision making.

3. *A Third Party.* Someone who perceives a need for help in a client system may be aware of the skills and resources available through consultation. This third party undertakes to bring the client and the consultant together. The initiative may be no more than a referral suggestion, or it may be as much as a formal, three-way meeting. The third party who is a power figure in the client system may simply retain the consultant and assign him or her to help where it seems to be needed.

Whether the potential consultant is internal or external makes some difference in this contact initiation. Typically the internal consultant knows more about the existence of difficulties or pain. The internal consultant also is not hampered by the problem of credible entry from the outside. In addition, referral by a third party is probably easier for the internal consultant because it is more convenient, more legitimate, and less expensive.

On the other hand, the external consultant often has an advantage because the client system finds it easier to share a problem with an outsider. In addition, when contact is established through referral by a third party, a link can be established between an outsider and a system. The client system also may assume greater expertise on the part of external consultants as compared with that of more familiar people inside the system.

Examples from Our Experiences

Ron: A frequent type of initial contact on the part of a potential client is a telephone call. Fairly typical is a call I had recently from someone at a professional school, asking if I would be interested in doing some kind of a program in professional and personal development and growth with doctoral candidates in a field internship program. After probing a bit to find out what he wanted, I decided he needed to think the situation through a little more before I could clearly respond about whether I would be an appropriate resource. I asked a number of questions and suggested that he write answers to the questions in a letter within the next day or two. I promised either to respond with a memo on what I might be able to do to meet the stated needs (as I understood them) or to make a referral to some other, more appropriate resource.

He wrote a good letter; and my response was a four-page, rather carefully developed memorandum, offering two alternative ideas about desirable outcomes and types of designs for helping. I included information on different levels of budget for the two alternatives and some of the initial data collection I would be asking him to do.

Gordon: Yes, telephone calls are a frequent first approach. I had a funny call the other day. A personnel director from a large pharmaceutical firm wanted me to meet with him and some others. When I asked the purpose of the meeting, he said, "Well, we need to have you talk with us about some OD work." When I asked about the kind of OD work, he said, "We'd just like to have you come and talk with us, and we'll pay a stipend for exploration." I discovered that the president of the firm was interested in assessing me, so we arranged to have lunch together.

Although the president of the firm was very affable and asked me some questions that weren't necessarily related to the project, the luncheon was definitely a testing of our mutual chemistry and my competency. The firm's OD director and the personnel director were there, ready to implement any further planning if the testing worked out. They called the next day with an O.K. to go ahead and do some exploratory planning.

Ron: Don't you think it is important when responding to these first contact initiatives to be very open in probing and sharing where you are?

Gordon: Yes, I think that's crucial. I recently received a letter from a community college that had issues concerning minority groups and faculty decision making. The college people wanted a problem-solving session of two days. I answered that letter very honestly and critically, explaining the impossibility of their expectations. I presented an alternative pattern with the probable conditions of contract and cost, but indicated that I didn't expect they would want to go ahead because this was going to be quite different from their objectives.

Surprisingly, they called back saying they were so impressed with my openness in confronting the unreality of their expectations that they wanted to go ahead with us rather than take a bid from one of the others who had accepted their assumptions. How about an example in which you have taken the initiative to try to get a client involved?

Ron: In one example, which was successful, we wrote two invitation letters, about a week apart, to a sample of potential clients—in this case, small businesses in the area.

The first letter was a warm-up, explaining who we were and some of our experiences with businesses similar to their own—in terms of new organization development procedures that were proving helpful in economic survival.

The second letter was a specific invitation to attend a three-hour luncheon session. At the luncheon we provided a sample "micro-event" with some input by us and some active participation by the guests, using models of goal setting and brainstorming, and identifying some of the major kinds of dilemmas that required their problem-solving efforts. The event ended with an opportunity for the guests to become involved in a consultative project, really a three-phase process of fact finding and consultation. We provided a handout on this process for them to take along and think about, and we promised to make a follow-up telephone call to see whether they would like to explore the opportunity.

Typically, out of the fifteen to twenty invitations, we would get eight to ten participants at the luncheon and two to four follow-up relationships that developed into client contracts.

Gordon: Very frequently, one of our successful initial contacts begins with participants we meet in a training activity who chat with us individually about their own situations. We suggest a follow-up contact to become acquainted with their situations and to explore the possibilities for following through on ideas they have acquired in the training activity. What kind of third-party entry situations come to your mind?

Ron: One of the most frequent problems in my experience is how to turn a coercive situation into a voluntary participation and learning activity. For example, there was the school administrator who asked us to work with his staff on ways to implement new accountability legislation that required the adoption and development of annual personnel review and assessment procedures. The challenge was how to convert this relatively negative entry situation into a collaboration in which the participants could become actively involved, see the payoff value to themselves, and learn that the consultant is not a tool of the administrator.

Gordon: Yes, in a recent situation, I had to work out a relationship difference between a state director, who was employing me, and the planning committee of the state staff, which was representing the client system. I began by being a third party, bringing the other two parties together to clarify some joint goals. Sometimes an entry situation is even more difficult when the president of the company assigns an internal consultant to "fix up that unproductive department."

Ron: "Fixing them up" is one of the biggest entry traps I experience. He who is ready to pay the bill is inviting me to enter his system, with no entry contacts with the proposed clients. I help the chief to understand that he will lose out by using this strategy. His subordinates will be angry with him for mandating our relationship and will be motivated to resist my efforts, so he will lose the potential benefit of my help. I usually get him to arrange a "what it would be like if" session with his staff and give the staff members the option of applying to work with me. The risk takers are ready, and those in the bandwagon group will come in two or three waves as they see the payoff for their peers.

Gordon: You remember the "budding-off process" that some of our Tavistock colleagues in London described. They wanted to engage a potential client through contact with a client with whom they had been successful. They had a visiting team of representatives from the potential client organization spend the morning with their counterparts in management, engineering, personnel, etc., in the organization that had experienced the successful intervention. Then they met with the visitors to see what practices the visitors had found attractive and interpreted what they had needed to do to achieve those improvements. Then they helped the visitors explore what *adaptations* might be relevant to their organization. They stressed that exact adoption (imitation) would not fit the visitors' situation, but that adaptations were feasible. Usually the day ended with the consultants scheduled to meet the visitors in their own system to try out some of the learnings.

Ron: I guess two of my general learnings about entry are that everybody is not ready to start to change at the same time and that those who will be expected to implement any change need to be involved in the entry process.

Gordon: And let's remember that the posture of the consultant needs to be that of "learner" even more than "seller."

Work Focus 2: Helping Identify and Clarify the Need for Change

After making contact, tentative entry into a working relationship includes some important processes of exploration. Usually it is a trap to assume that the problem as presented by the potential client is the core of the problem. The most effective posture for the consultant, we believe, is that of co-explorer of the problem concern; the consultant should assume that the client system needs to achieve insight just as much as he or she needs to gain diagnostic awareness. Thus, the second work focus involves the consultant in helping the potential client to probe and clarify his or her understanding of the problem, thereby achieving a wider perspective of its causes.

Sometimes the potential consultant functions as a legitimized listener and asker of questions; sometimes he or she is an inquiry expert with tools for conducting an assessment of needs. Sometimes a potential helper must cope with a lack of sensitivity to the need for change, a lack of sense of responsibility, or an inability to enter into or put energy into any kind of change effort. These problems may require the consultant to call the attention of the potential client to the ways in which other systems have identified and worked on similar problems. Often there is a need for group interviewing in which individuals occupying different positions in the system stimulate one another's articulation of perceptions of relevant issues and problems. Such openness can be legitimized by the objectivity of the interview situation and by the questions asked by the consultant as interviewer.

At this stage the internal consultant usually is better prepared to probe, listen, and clarify; but probing is likely to create defensiveness because of his or her status as a member of the organizational family. The external consultant has the disadvantage of lacking the context and history of the particular system and its operational problems, but the advantage of third-party objectivity.

Examples from Our Experiences

Ron: The group interview is one of the most valuable ways to help potential clients identify and clarify their needs. For a recent community project, in which an interagency council wanted to explore problems of poor communication and cooperation, we conducted a series of five group interviews. There were six or seven people in each group; and each group was heterogeneous, with the members coming from different agencies. In these interviews the participants stimulated one another, and their interactions gave us a great deal of data about the issues of communication and collaboration.

Gordon: I often use quick, anonymous, written surveys with key management people. Then I get them together for a feedback session in which we share, probe their interpretations, and amplify what has been revealed in the survey statements.

Ron: Another helpful technique is asking a small, representative group to simulate being an outside committee making an assessment of the organization. During the simulated visit, the observers describe what they see that pleases them as some of the strengths of the organization and what they are sorry to see and wish could be changed in order for the organization to function more effectively. This kind of listing, based on brainstorming from a perspective of outside objectivity, is very helpful in getting out the data.

Gordon: One of the things I find inadequate about most needs-assessment techniques is that they tend to reinforce a negative, critical posture toward "what's wrong," rather than a proactive posture of exploring images of "what would be desirable," "what are possible alternatives."

Ron: I have found Kurt Lewin's principles of action reseach really basic at this stage. If we can get the potential client system involved in collecting the diagnostic data, this becomes a major stimulus toward self-discovery and toward acceptance of the data as credible.

Work Focus 3: Exploring the Readiness for Change Effort

This is important, mutually shared work in which the consultant explores the readiness of the client system to devote time, energy, and the committed involvement of appropriate people to a problem-solving process. The client system, on the other hand, explores the capability, sensitivity, credibility, and trustworthiness of the potential consultant.

Almost any type of change effort requires changes in the assignment priorities of personnel and the commitment of management to additional tasks. The time commitments of the inside team members must be clarified. At this point it may be difficult for some managers to visualize and accept the potential payoffs of the extra effort, so any added work may be seen as a disruption of an already overloaded work schedule.

Examples from Our Experiences

Gordon: I always feel a big gain in confidence at this point if I've been able to identify one or two on-the-ball insiders who are eager to learn professional skills and who can sell management on the long-term payoff for the system if these personnel can be given the time and support to work with me.

Ron: Yes, and it also makes a difference if management can be helped to accept off-site sessions or a weekend workshop or a series of two-hour, on-the-job sessions as a normal part of the process of introducing innovative changes that will affect "the bottom line."

Gordon: I think the key point is to be open and positive, rather than defensive, about the kinds of needed activities that might emerge during the problem-solving effort.

Work Focus 4: Exploring the Potential for Working Together

Each of the parties explores and tests the potential for an effective working relationship. Familiarity can lead a client system to stereotyped preconceptions of an internal consultant's particular responses, and these preconceptions may be quite incorrect. The potential client may have conscious or unconscious fears about the difficulties of withdrawing from a working relationship with an internal consultant, whereas terminating a contract with an external consultant may be seen as easier to accomplish. Frequently the external consultant is more readily able to clarify the nature of available resources. Many external consultants consider it important to propose a period of testing for compatibility before making mutual commitments for a long-term working relationship.

Examples from Our Experiences

Ron: To explore readiness for change, we have found it helpful with several clients to develop, with their help, a list of good reasons for *not* having the time or motivation or inclination to get involved in a change effort, and a parallel list of reasons *for* becoming involved. We make this into a check list, asking clients to check the items on both sides that are true of themselves, to give some value weighting to the most important ones on each side, and then to use the list as a basis for discussing where they are. This kind of procedure legitimizes any hidden agendas of resistance and gets things out in the open for sharing and decision making.

Gordon: Frequently I ask the person who is negotiating with me to identify all the key people who would be involved in collaborating with my consultation and to convene them in an ad hoc session. This allows me to have an open discussion with these people about who I am and why I've been invited in, and it encourages them to ask any clarifying questions, make any statements of doubt or support, etc.

Ron: I had quite a time recently in a large hospital. I was exploring and probing to discover who the client really would be. It was a chance to meet with the different clusters of personnel, giving them a chance to examine me and to determine what kind of control they would have over the process of working and what my expectations would be if we worked together. I had to meet with about six such clusters before going back to the administrator to clarify and define potential working relationships.

Gordon: I frequently try a kind of microcosm of what working together would be like. Usually I involve people in some activities, some brainstorming, and a little bit of process observation; and I offer some input about typical activities done in an organization development program such as the one they are considering. This helps to surface differences in orientation, readiness, and commitment.

PHASE II: FORMULATING A CONTRACT AND ESTABLISHING A HELPING RELATIONSHIP

The four work focuses of Phase I should produce at least a tentative decision on the part of both consultant and client either to discontinue the exploration or to move toward some kind of agreement about the nature, objectives, and conditions of a working relationship. We have identified three focuses of work in the second phase.

Work Focus 5: Identifying Desired Outcomes

It is not enough just to agree that there is a problem or that a change is desirable. In clarifying a potential working relationship, it is important to explore what kinds of outcomes are possible and desirable if the working relationship is successful. For example, a client's desired outcomes might include an increase in profits, improvement of its public image, or a change in the motivation of its workers or in the working relationship between its supervisors and their subordinates. This certainly will not constitute the final statement of objectives, but it should provide a basis for the mutual understanding needed to formulate a contract.

In this type of work, the internal consultant has a better grasp of feasibility and need, but may have too much of a negative problem orientation. The external consultant may be better able to achieve a wider perspective on possible goals and desirable outcomes.

Examples from Our Experiences

Gordon: With more and more clients, I'm finding it worthwhile to spend quite a bit of initial time trying to get concrete about what changes they would like in the way they are operating. Although the goal setting typically comes later in a consulting relationship, it is important to probe clients for the concrete outcomes they want from any kind of developmental or change effort, which usually means stretching their thinking.

Ron: I certainly agree with you. Recently I met with representatives of a large church to explore whether we might work together. I asked them to play the roles that leaders of the church would have in five years and to make a list of the things that pleased them concerning the progress made in those five years. They became very involved in this listing and began to clarify and considerably change their ideas about what they were after.

Ron: Another challenge is to help the client group explore "whose desired outcomes" should be considered. I was working with a group of school administrators who had defined their priorities for quality education in the classroom for the next fall. They were ready to work on planning for implementation when I asked them to stand up and "let the others have their seats." I explained that they were to act as parents and call out "through the mouths of parents" the quality education priorities. Thirteen new items came out. Then I asked them to invite a student into each seat, and they called out priorities through the mouths of students. They then put on their own "hats" and prioritized again. Over half of the items were from their new lists. In most cases we need to ask the question "Whose desired outcomes need to be included?"

Work Focus 6: Determining Who Should Do What

The client has a strong need to know how much time, energy, and commitment the consultant is ready to put into a helping relationship. The consultant has a strong need for clarification about who should be involved, what kinds of activity would be feasible, what kind of support could be expected from the top power structure, what kind of financial and time commitments would be made, and how the contract would be terminated. At this stage it is crucial to determine who the client system is, particularly to discover whether there is a difference between the client system and the individual or office that pays the bills.

Examples from Our Experiences

Gordon: "Who is really the client?" is one of the toughest and most important questions every consultant has to deal with and answer. It is so easy to be trapped into assuming it's the person who pays you.

Ron: Yes, I have a client now, a CEO, who wants me to do team building with his six department heads. Clearly, they will have to become included in my client system; and if I find this requires working with some of their subordinates, this will extend the client system again.

Gordon: I've come to believe that usually my definition of my client keeps changing and expanding during the course of my work with a client system. Is my client those I am going to interact with, or do I include those who will be impacted directly by my consulting efforts?

Ron: I guess that dilemma is one reason why I have come to think of my relationship to a *client system* rather than my relationship to the person with whom I negotiated my contract.

Work Focus 7: Clarifying Time Perspective and Accountability

Another part of formulating the contract includes clarifying the projected time period allowed for accomplishing the desired outcomes and the evaluation procedures to be used in assessing progress toward the desired outcomes. This time perspective may include agreement about milestones at which the progress of the working relationship will be reviewed and decisions about continuation or termination will be made.

Because of his or her ongoing relationship with the client system, the internal consultant probably has a more difficult time arriving at some criteria for evaluation and termination or continuation. However, the internal consultant certainly should be closer to the flow of data about the success or lack of success of the helping efforts. The external consultant may have an easier time proposing objective evaluation procedures and obtaining the client's commitments to provide the necessary data for evaluation. But the external consultant usually works with the time perspective of a much more ad hoc relationship, with accountability being expected much sooner.

Examples from Our Experiences

Gordon: I'm finding that more and more clients are ready to develop written agreements. Frequently there is a discussion with certain members of a client system about who will do what and the timing, etc., but the contract about financial arrangements is with somebody else in a different office. This can bring about some real problems. For example, recently we had worked out the arrangements for a three-day workshop for the top executives of a national government agency. But then the agency postponed the event because the contract office had some questions that hadn't been answered and some forms that had to be signed.

Ron: For things such as time schedules and commitments, we have found it helpful to develop a first draft of the contract and then to say, in essence, "I need to check this out with colleagues who are going to be involved, and I would like you to do the same. Because both parties tend to forget some things that become very important later, we need to have a critical review before finalizing anything."

Gordon: Another important aspect of contracting is having a tryout or pilot project of limited duration and magnitude before asking either party to go into something larger and long term. For example, in a recent team-building program with a large school system, we asked for a small pilot project with two buildings, with careful observation and documentation by some internal staff members in order to assess and review the feasibility of the design and the results that might be expected. This relieved a lot of pressure, provided some good testing on feasibility, and was a good basis for developing a working relationship; it made a larger, more comprehensive design workable and fundable.

PHASE III: IDENTIFYING PROBLEMS THROUGH DIAGNOSTIC ANALYSIS

Processes of entry and contract formulation involve preliminary diagnostic activity, readiness for change, and the dynamics of a working relationship. This is all preliminary to the much more intensive diagnostic work and planning for action required in any successful consultative relationship.

Work Focus 8: Using Force-Field Diagnosis

Force-field diagnosis is a model or method for identifying the forces that impede movement toward current goals and the forces that facilitate such movement (see the force-field diagram in Figure 1). The client system is likely to encounter problems in providing opportunities for the data collection and staff involvement that are requested by the consultant, and the consultant is responsible for being focused and sensitive in fact-finding efforts. The consultant is faced with the responsibility or helping the client to interpret the causes of problems and the implications for change.

The internal consultant, usually aware of the existence of diagnostic data, is able to recommend appropriate targets for data collection; but being part of the organizational family is more likely to create defensiveness and resistance. Normally it is easier for the external consultant to request unfamiliar types of data collection and to use new methods and tools.

Examples from Our Experiences

Gordon: The force-field diagram is an important tool in helping clients gain perspective on the numerous blocks and inhibitions as well as supports and resources in their operations. Recently, when working with the staff of a government agency, I put two sheets of newsprint on the wall and diagramed the force field. From the brainstorming of the group members, I was able to list on one sheet the supports and resources they had for accomplishing their work goal. On the other sheet I listed the restraints and blocks they identified from their experiences in trying to get things done. In each case they indicated whether the support or the block came from inside themselves (that is, from certain norms and traditions of the group) or from traditions and characteristics of their environment, such as the budget, regulations, and physical setting. Then they prioritized the resources they were inadequately utilizing and the blocks they should eliminate.

Ron: A different use for the force field, applicable in the phase-four examination of planning, is to write a projected goal at the top of the force-field diagram and identify the potential resources and restraints that affect movement toward the goal. This provides data for planning.

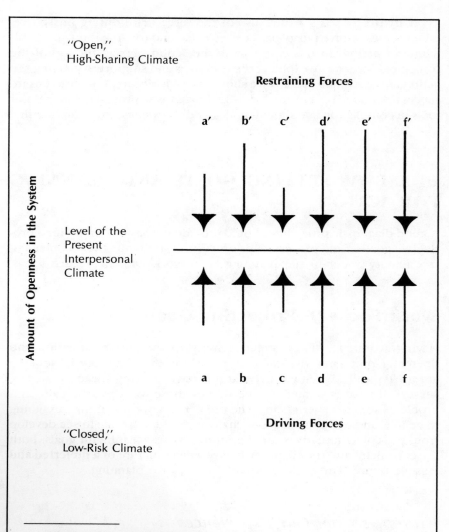

From "Kurt Lewin's 'Force Field Analysis'" (p. 112) by M.S. Spier, in The 1973 Annual Handbook for Group Facilitators by J.E. Jones and J.W. Pfeiffer (Eds.), 1973, San Diego, California: University Associates. Reprinted by permission of the publisher.

Figure 1. Force-Field Diagram

Gordon: There's a third use of the force field: during phase five, when some action strategy has been selected and the task is one of mobilizing for action. In this case I write the action steps at the top of the force-field diagram. We look at the resources and supports for taking the action and the kinds of traps we should be sensitive to in order to ensure success. All three uses of the force-field diagnostic procedure are helpful tools in consultation and should be clearly differentiated from one another.

PHASE IV: SETTING GOALS AND PLANNING FOR ACTION

A good diagnostic procedure should provide the basic warmup for a productive goal-setting process. This process must include the complementary activity of step-by-step planning of the work required to reach a goal.

Work Focus 9: Projecting Goals

Having acquired a diagnostic sensitivity to the current situation and operating problems, the client is ready for the challenge of looking ahead. Typically, when we arrive at this stage, looking ahead is aided by surveys of what is wanted and needed by those we serve, the pains and problems we are experiencing, the predictions of what things are going to be like, and our own values—what we would most like to see develop from possible alternatives for the future. To set meaningful goals, both the consultant and the client must have a clear picture of a preferred and feasible future. This picture provides a basis for planning.

Examples from Our Experiences

Ron: An interesting illustration of projecting long-range goals is a recent situation I experienced involving a large national organization. The organization's planning committee started with current goals and a survey of goal priorities and projected eight areas from which goals needed to be developed. The committee commissioned a team to review data on trends and a projection written by a group of futurists and then, from their analyses, to project three or four alternative and possible futures. These alternative-future statements became the basis for goal-setting workshops throughout the organization, in which leaders identified their preferences and explained their rationales and the efforts needed to create the chosen futures.

Gordon: Often I find it helpful to begin by providing a client with input on some major trends in society—economic, political, social, etc. I did this recently with a state mental health department, and the staff members were stimulated to look at the relevance of societal trends for their own departmental future. The staff members projected specific images of their operation five years hence, taking into account the trends of which they had become aware, the developmental trends in their own organization, and their vision of a future optimized with their own evaluations of good practices.

Ron: Yes, I think there is great value in helping clients develop EDT (events, developments, trends) projects as ongoing activities. My futurist colleague, Ed Lindaman, referred to these as "the future nipping at our heels." In one of my client systems, a volunteer EDT group meets for a brown-bag lunch every two weeks to report what the members have learned from their scans of newspapers, magazines, journals, and papers given at meetings. Then they brainstorm the potential implications of these trends for their company and for their departments. The documentor of each meeting gives the data to the strategic-planning group. It is highly valued.

Gordon: The creative generating of potential goals has to be followed by a disciplined procedure of selecting priorities. I have been amazed at the degree of consensus that typically emerges when the priority-voting process narrows seventy-five to a hundred alternative goal ideas down to a dozen top priorities. Your book with Ed is very helpful in guiding this procedure.[1]

---

[1]*Choosing the Future You Prefer* by R. Lippitt and E.B. Lindaman, 1979, Bethesda, MD: Development Publications.

Work Focus 10: Planning for Action and Involvement

When planning the implementation of meaningful goals, the key to success is devising a sequence of steps toward each goal (identifying specifically *what* should be done). Often the plan stipulates that simultaneous steps be taken by different persons or groups. Criteria or evidence that each step has been achieved must be identified, so that the client has clear indications either that the right path is being pursued or that the direction needs to be changed. These criteria also should provide a basis for celebrating success, which keeps motivation alive.

One of the most critical and neglected phases of planning is an anticipatory rehearsal. It helps to answer the question of *who* (from inside or outside the system) should be involved in order for a plan of action to have the best probability of success. Once these people have been identified, the question of *how* to involve them must be answered. This sets up new planning sequences and new goals that are concentrated on involvement strategy.

The internal consultant probably has more knowledge and more access to knowledge about the potential resource value of people and units that should be involved at various stages in the problem-solving action. However, it is also more difficult for the internal consultant to request the participation of top power figures in the client system and the involvement of parts of the system that are uncommitted but crucial. The external consultant often has great leverage with respect to involvement.

Examples from Our Experiences

Ron: Using a rehearsal procedure is the best way I know of improving the quality of action and, therefore, the probability of success. One of my current clients is using temporary task forces to explore innovative improvements in the quality of the product. A task force typically has five or six meetings before it reports its recommendations to management. The last meeting is a rehearsal of the presentation given by two or three of the task-force members, with someone taking the role of manager and the remaining members making observations about the performance and giving feedback on ideas for improving the presentation. Often a task force will go through five or six such rehearsals to "get it right." Our estimate is that this rehearsal procedure increases the probability of success from 30 to 70 percent.

   Gordon: The idea of celebrating progress is so crucial and is almost universally neglected. In so many cases the length of time between start and completion is so long and full of problems that morale goes down, energy is lost, and a positive perspective about achieving the goals is lost. I was working with a new-product-development team last week. The members of the team couldn't expect real payoff in less than a year or two. I had them brainstorm all the ways they could celebrate or get recognition when they could identify a step of progress. They listed eleven ways and were in a very positive mood as they tackled their task.

PHASE V: TAKING ACTION AND CYCLING FEEDBACK

The payoff of consulting lies in successful action and in the continuity of long-term gains after the first bursts of energy and effort are expended. We have identified three work focuses of the critical implementation phase.

Work Focus 11: Taking Successful Action

In the fifth phase of consulting, the consultant is responsible for helping people to develop the skills necessary to increase their chances of achieving success in the actions they take. He or she also must support the celebrations of small successes on a step-by-step path of action. The major motivation for continuing effort comes from frequent experiences of successful movement on a defined path that leads somewhere. The effective consultant also works with key parts of the client system to coordinate multiple activities and the involvement of individuals and units.

   The internal consultant is better able to observe the action that takes place and to assess the levels of skill needed for this action. However, the external consultant probably has greater leverage for introducing skill-development activities and for initiating sessions designed to examine progress and to review process issues.

Examples from Our Experiences

Ron: The opportunity and responsibility for helping the client celebrate has become increasingly important to me. A recent example is my work with a group of thirteen compensatory education teams, made up of teachers, aides, and volunteers from center-city schools.

The members of each team projected some goals of what they would like to have happen in the classroom and in their own performance within six months. They developed a series of criteria of progress toward their goals, and through brainstorming they decided to stop at least every two or three weeks to check on evidence of progress. They identified fourteen different ways in which they might have meaningful celebrations, ranging all the way from going to the principal to explain how well they were getting along, to food celebrations in their classrooms, to having a drink together after school.

It has been exciting to hear about their various celebrations and the ways in which these events have provided a continuing basis for group cohesiveness and motivation.

Gordon: I think the whole notion of anticipatory preparation for action tends to be neglected. Rehearsal or simulation is very important, and I try to help most of my client systems work on anticipatory preparation.

A departmental group I was working with in a large company arrived at the point of needing involvement, support, and sanction from top management. After briefing me in the role of top manager, the members of the group practiced their presentation, using feedback from me and from one another for improving their skills of presentation. They made a lot of improvements and felt good when they were successful.

Ron: Various kinds of process interventions can help groups to improve their action by stopping and looking at how they are doing and how they might be improving their action. We made very active use of stop sessions while working with the ward teams of a large psychiatric facility on improving their clinical decision making and planning in regard to individual patients. After the teams had been working for fifteen or twenty minutes on a particular case conference, we would intervene for a minute to have all of the members complete a brief, stop-session check sheet, rating their feelings of how well they were being listened to, how well they were listening to others, and how they were doing in decision making. They shared their data, becoming consultants for themselves with ideas for improving their operating procedure, and within five to eight minutes moved ahead to continue their work, typically with many evidences of improvement.

Work Focus 12: Evaluating and Guiding Feedback

Using appropriate procedures to elicit feedback about progress and to involve the necessary people in the assessment of this feedback is a crucial part of the consultant's role during the action phase. This continuing assessment of the consequences of action can save more dollars, hours, and energy than any other of the consultant's helping efforts.

With the advantage of being in closer touch with the change procedures, the internal consultant usually is more able to secure feedback at strategic points, but there may also be greater motivation to hide problems from him or her. The external consultant can more easily introduce new methodologies for obtaining feedback data and can legitimately convene analysis and feedback sessions with appropriate personnel.

Examples from Our Experiences

Ron: One important aspect of getting feedback is to plan for early-warning clues that action is "getting off the beam." The early work on feedback involves sending out a beam and getting a bounce back showing how many degrees the action is off course in order to make corrections. I have one client, a college, in which the faculty and senior-student advisors use "early-warning cards" on which they jot down symptoms that might be clues that a student is a potential dropout. The early-warning cards go to the student-services office, where they can be followed up. This early-warning system has remarkable sensitivity in identifying potential dropouts.

Gordon: One of the most important aspects of getting and using feedback is the kind of design that exists for "feedback on the feedback." Any time we request feedback data from people, we are entering into an ethical commitment to give back some kind of feedback on whether their messages were heard and what was done with their data. One mistake many leaders make is to assume they are expected to "do what the feedback says" rather than to use the data as important intelligence, along with other data, to think and decide creatively as leaders.

Ron: Certainly unless we give feedback about the feedback, there will be a negative assumption that the data went into a file or wastebasket or was used to exploit and manipulate. Most of us have a long history of filing our questionnaires, with no evidence our ideas were listened to or had any influence.

Work Focus 13: Revising Action and Mobilizing Additional Resources

Feedback is only helpful if it is used rapidly in re-examining goals, revising action strategies, and perhaps prompting decisions concerning the mobilization of additional resources and changes of assignments and roles.

The internal consultant may be in a better position to be aware of needed but unused resources, at least those within the system. But the external consultant has an advantage in using the data to confront blockages and resistance to effective action. In addition, the external consultant probably has a better perspective from which to suggest alternative courses of action and the need for external resources.

Examples from Our Experiences

Ron: Collecting evaluation data is really a waste of time unless some planning and energy are put into processing and using the findings, rewarding those who have made relevant efforts, and revising and improving plans for the next stages of action.

I had an interesting client situation with a school system and a PTA. I had been helping them to collaborate on developing a procedure for the sharing of decision making, goal setting, and action planning by school administrators, board members, teachers, parents, and students. The evaluation procedure involved interviews with each of these subgroups conducted by trained pairs of teachers, students, parents, or administrators. The data focused on feelings about the problems, successes, and issues that had been experienced. The important feature was the feedback teams, each consisting of a parent, teacher, student, and administrator. In a series of sessions, table groups of five to seven listened to the findings, presented one or two at a time by the feedback teams. The groups brainstormed implications for improvement of communication and collaboration, reported these, and at each session arrived at some priorities for next steps and some conclusions about the values and strengths of what they had been doing.

Gordon: It's also desirable for a consultant to get feedback about how people are reacting to him or her. After a day or two with clients, I give them a little check sheet to record their reactions to my efforts and suggest ways in which I might be more helpful. The clients seem to like this, and it certainly gives me some helpful data for revising my efforts.

Ron: An evaluation issue that comes up fairly frequently is the pressure to cut funds that presumably were allocated in the budget for documentation and evaluation. This has made me more sensitive about getting a clear statement about evaluation into the consultation contract and keeping it before the client as a continuing value and responsibility. Of course, one key is to demonstrate how helpful evaluation can be.

Gordon: I believe documentation is one of the most neglected aspects of the work of consultants with clients. Without good documentation of what has gone on, it is difficult to pass on to internal consultants many of the designs and activities that have worked well and should be continued. It is also very difficult to report to policy boards and to outside funding sources what has been done and how helpful it has been. And, finally, most organizations that have a successful development program or develop innovations in their ways of operation should be responsible enough to share these learnings with other agencies needing this type of resource.

PHASE VI: COMPLETING THE CONTRACT (CONTINUITY, SUPPORT, AND TERMINATION)

The greatest problem with many consultation efforts is that the changes achieved often succumb to one of three pitfalls: They are short term and followed by regression to old patterns; they are fragile and lead to poor continuity of the new status; or they are marked by the growth of counter-reactions that must be coped with quickly in order to guarantee their continuity. Many consultation designs do not include a plan for follow-up support or provisions for gradual termination of the consultant's help and installation within the system of the successfully used resources.

Work Focus 14: Designing Continuity Supports

The designing of support systems for the successful continuity of change effort is perhaps the most significant test of the consultant's competence. Sometimes the result of this effort is a plan for a continuing review of events, including and involving a wide circle of personnel from the client system. Often there is a program of support conference calls with the consultant to check deadlines. Another type of support design involves documenting and reporting success through publication and professional meetings.

The internal consultant is present on a continuing basis to observe where and when additional support is needed to maintain the new structure, roles, or processes. The external consultant, on the other hand, is in a strong position to negotiate reviews and to provide skill training for the involvement of new personnel or inside change agents.

Work Focus 15: Establishing Termination Plans

A professional responsibility and goal of most consultants is to become progressively unnecessary. Consultants design for this in various ways, including:

- Training an insider to take over the functions initiated by the consultant;
- Setting a series of dates for decreasing the budget and the involvement of the consultant;
- Having a termination celebration for the final product of a collaborative effort, such as a publication; and
- Establishing a minimal periodic maintenance plan, such as an annual review session.

The key notion is that every consultation relationship must have some plan for a healthy, mutually satisfying termination of the working relationship. Established early, this plan helps to guide many intervention decisions during all phases of consultation.

Examples from Our Experiences

Ron: I have found temporary task forces most helpful in continuing organization development. Each has a convener, an agenda, and a time sequence of meetings. Usually before discontinuing my active relationship, I sit in on at least the first session of each task force and work with the internal coordinator on plans for receiving reports and reconvening the group. In one such situation, each task force committed publicly to a consultation period with me to present its plans for work.

Gordon: One important continuity procedure is to develop a close working relationship with one or more persons inside the system who have been designated as having the continuing role of consultant or change agent. I work extensively with them during my time with the client system, and later I am available to them by telephone or I make periodic visitations on their request to help support the work.

Ron: The potential of periodic telephone consultations is not appreciated enough by most consultants. Currently, in one situation in which I have been working with teams in several branches of the same agency, each team has a telephone amplifier box. On a monthly basis we have a conference call with each team, with the members sitting around the amplifier box. This procedure allows us to have discussions of progress, successes, and ideas for next steps.

FINAL COMMENT

We have found this framework of phases and work focuses useful in our own consulting practice and in helping many internal and external consultants to clarify their roles and guide their intervention decisions. In the next two chapters, we examine in more detail the multiple roles of consultation and the challenges and dilemmas encountered in making appropriate intervention decisions.

REFERENCE

Lippitt, R., & Lindaman, E.B. (1979). *Choosing the future you prefer.* Bethesda, MD: Development Publications.

3

Interventions: Making Decisions and Ensuring Quality

A consultant can be evaluated according to the range and quality of his or her repertoire of interventions. The repertoire needs to be large enough to enable the consultant to provide appropriate help to a variety of client systems coping with a wide range of problems. Included in this repertoire should be behavioral skills, learning tools and activities, problem-solving designs, and strategies of planned change. In this chapter we want to share our learnings about building such a repertoire, making intervention decisions, and using various resources and supports to ensure the quality of consultative behaviors.

DECISION-MAKING INVENTORY

One crucial resource is a conceptual framework within which to organize one's thinking about types of interventions. The consultant needs to determine what specific challenges he or she should be prepared to respond to and which interventions would be appropriate for each of these challenges. In the following inventory we have summarized some questions that a consultant should answer in order to determine whether he or she possesses the skills necessary for a high-quality repertoire. These questions have been divided into categories according to the phase of consultation to which they apply. Later in the chapter we present some ways of developing the consulting skills implied in these questions.

INVENTORY OF INTERVENTION DECISIONS

Phase I: Engaging in Initial Contact and Entry

Critical Intervention Questions

1. How can I legitimize for clients their sharing of pain, problems, and sense of failure without also stimulating their defensiveness?
2. How can I ask probing questions and not mobilize feelings of irritation and hostility toward me?
3. How can I listen to and encourage the unloading of problems without appearing to accept projections of blame and premature ideas about what is causing the exposed problem?
4. How can I demonstrate expertise and establish my credibility as a potential source of help without creating dependence and an expectation that I will solve the problem?
5. How can I explain readiness to work on change without appearing to assume (before diagnosis) that a lot of change is needed?
6. How can I bring up and explore questions of compatibility without sounding too clinical, doubtful, or demanding?
7. How can I communicate my relevant experience and training without sounding as if I am giving a sales pitch?
8. How can I be reassuring without being interpreted as saying the problem is minor or can be easily and quickly solved?

Phase II: Formulating a Contract and Establishing a Helping Relationship

Critical Intervention Questions

1. How can I explore potential traps and misunderstandings with clients without appearing negative?
2. How can I strike a balance between making clients' responsibilities and commitments seem too heavy (at this early stage) and letting them make false assumptions about the amount of work that I will expect them to do?
3. How can I test compatibility and skills collaboration without entering into irreversible commitments?
4. How can I clarify the level of my commitment of time and energy without appearing to sell myself or have inflexible standards?

5. How can I clarify some limitation of my resources without creating loss of confidence in me?

6. How can I realistically communicate my available time and energy without discouraging the client?

7. How can I work for involvement of appropriate parts of the system without antagonizing the "in" group?

8. How can I stretch the necessary time perspective of the contract without appearing to promote more work for myself?

9. How can I write the commitment about the participation of top management without creating defensiveness and game playing?

10. How can financial terms be definite and yet flexible in response to changes in conditions (for example, handling new critical problems that are discovered or dealing with conflicts that arise)?

11. How can the client and I define outcomes and accountability without creating traps and limitations?

12. How can a division of labor be defined without too much rigidity and without scaring people?

Phase III: Identifying Problems Through Diagnostic Analysis

Critical Intervention Questions

1. How can I help people in the client system to be open and to question their assumptions about the causes of their problems?

2. How can I persuade them to accept the need for objective fact finding to supplement their own assumptions?

3. How can I introduce perspective about the time that is needed without discouraging them?

4. How can I obtain their understanding of and commitment to the time and energy that will be required of them?

5. How can I involve them enough in the diagnostic data-collection process so that they will feel ownership of the data and accept the validity of these data?

6. How can I arrange for people in the appropriate parts of the client system to review the data and draw implications for action?

7. How can I divert people's attention from working on the causes of their pain or problems and help them to focus instead on data about needs and readiness for change and images of potential desired outcomes?

Phase IV: Setting Goals and Planning for Action

Critical Intervention Questions

1. How can I create a psychological readiness in people to freely imagine alternative futures?
2. How can I free them enough from inhibiting assumptions about adjusting, predicting, and feasibility to project a desired future based on their values?
3. How can I prevent them from choosing goals before they have tested alternatives for probable consequences?
4. How can I confront the tendency to involve too few members of the system in goal setting and planning?
5. How can I press for concreteness and measurability in goal statements without evoking a negative reaction?
6. How can I stimulate an interest in step-by-step goal planning instead of a preoccupation with big, long-term perspectives?
7. How can I support planning for evaluation as part of planning for implementation?
8. How can I help with reality testing of plans?
9. How can I help clients to explore the possible side effects and traps that are part of planning?
10. How can I push for personnel commitments of time, effort, and acceptance of deadlines without creating resistance and flight?
11. How can I stimulate clients to consider the need for and use of resources beyond themselves?
12. How can I plan for my withdrawal and the development of internal resources to replace my functions?

Phase V: Taking Action and Cycling Feedback

Critical Intervention Questions

1. How can I present to clients the value of action rehearsal so that it will be accepted?
2. How can I present and demonstrate the value of skill training?
3. How can I communicate that effective involvement, briefing techniques, and preparation for implementation should replace the assumption that good intentions and acceptance of goals are adequate?

4. How can I confront the weakness of an authoritarian strategy with a process based on voluntary involvement?

5. How can I deal with the dependence of clients who want me to use my expertise to produce the action?

6. How can I introduce procedures for obtaining feedback on each action step and for using the data?

7. How can I support the use of other resources as an evidence of strength rather than weakness?

8. How can I introduce and support celebration of milestones of progress?

9. How can I help those who are taking action to understand the importance of support systems and to use one another for support, reinforcement, and debriefing?

10. How can I support the commitment to document the action and the consequences?

Phase VI: Completing the Contract (Continuity, Support, and Termination)

Critical Intervention Questions

1. How can I deal objectively with my own conflicting inclinations to see "all the help the client still needs" and also to move on to do "new and exciting things"?

2. How can I involve the client in setting goals that increase self-direction and internal support?

3. How can I make appropriate commitments for periodic support as needed?

4. How can I confront and support the need for specific deadlines on progress checkpoints, the need for renewal, and similar needs?

5. How can I find ways to provide support from a distance?

6. How can I support plans for documentation and evaluation?

7. How can I support plans for continuing internal personnel development and internal change-agent functions?

8. How can I help to clarify the client's understanding of ongoing and potential needs for external help and appropriate procedures for securing such help?

9. How can the client and I appropriately celebrate the completion of our contract?

INTERVENTION MATRIX

The Intervention Matrix (see Figure 2) offers a way to keep track of an intervention. The matrix deals with the two major dimensions of every intervention: its *focus* and its *purpose*. The focus may be an individual, a group, or a larger system such as an organization or community. The four main purposes, which are derived from the six phases of consultation presented in Chapter 2, are "unfreezing" the client, fostering change and/or learning, maintaining and supporting changes and learning that have been accomplished, and terminating the contract. Each of these four main purposes is divided into subcategories representing the steps to be taken to accomplish that purpose.

PURPOSE OF INTERVENTION	FOCUS OF INTERVENTION		
	Individual	Group	Organization (or Macrosystem)
I. "Unfreezing" the client 1. *Initiating* contact, entry credibility, start-up			
2. *Responding* to probes about competence, purpose, relevance			
3. *Initiating* contract, exploring, proposing, negotiating			
4. *Responding* to queries about cost, commitment, time			
5. *Initiating* diagnostic exploration, needs assessment			
6. *Responding* to problem and diagnostic statements, assumptions			
II. Change Work, Learning 1. *Initiating* goal setting, alternatives, value clarification			
2. *Responding* to probes about direction, change intentions, expectations			

Figure 2. Intervention Matrix

3. *Initiating* action planning, designing for learning			
4. *Responding* to probes about dependency, responsibility, help needs			
5. *Initiating* skill development, action risking, learning projects			
6. *Responding* to help requests, flight tendencies			
III. Maintaining, Supporting Change Efforts, Learnings 1. *Initiating* support for effort, motivation, commitments			
2. *Responding* to needs, requests for support			
3. *Initiating* evaluation, feedback cycles, renewal designs, celebration			
4. Responding to requests for evaluation, legitimization, reinforcement			
IV. Terminating, Separating, Withdrawing, Transferring 1. *Initiating* transfer to internal resources, to "back-home" situation			
2. *Responding* to dependence needs, autonomy postures			
3. *Initiating* designs for documentation, spread, "ripple" effects, publication			
4. *Responding* to pressures for privacy, lack of sharing, premature dissemination			

Figure 2 (continued). Intervention Matrix

OTHER FACTORS THAT AFFECT SUCCESS

When a "critical moment" arises in an intervention, the consultant who can think of the greatest number of possible reactions is most likely to behave effectively. However, although a large repertoire of ideas, strategies, and techniques increases the probability of a successful endeavor, it does not ensure success. Other factors are also important, and several of these are discussed below.

The Quality of Decision Making

Having alternative behaviors at one's disposal is important, but having a framework of values or criteria for making choices between or among alternatives is equally important. For example, when a consultant senses that a client resists changing his or her authoritarian style, that consultant needs to be able to choose a response that fosters collaboration, support, and acceptance and to reject those alternative responses that would make the client feel guilty, defensive, or angry. When a consultant chooses an inappropriate response, he or she jeopardizes progress.

Rosenberg (1951) revealed these interesting dilemmas that face the consultant:

- A consultant who develops deep empathy for the client generates fewer causal hypotheses about the client's needs and motivations.
- The consultant who identifies deeply with and becomes an advocate for the client is often a poor resource of help. Under these circumstances the consultant is unable to generate alternative ideas for problem-solving action and has more limited value criteria for choosing appropriate ways of helping.

In addition, the following important issues must be dealt with. Each represents still another decision-making dilemma that challenges a consultant as he or she develops and uses diagnostic resources:

1. *Time and Energy.* The consultant must determine how much time and energy should be invested in an initial data-collection or diagnostic phase. This investment can be great, or the consultant can elect to move quickly into some pilot actions and develop diagnostic information from observations of what happens.

2. *Client Involvement in Data-Collection Activities.* The consultant must decide to what degree the client or client group should be

involved in the actual data-collection activities. Data-collection experts have more technical tools and skills at their disposal. However, data collected by experts are often rejected by the client because ownership and validity have not been established. This approach can be contrasted to that of the action-research model, which involves the client system in defining the inquiry questions, developing the procedures to be used, and helping to collect and process the information.

    3. *Sharing of Data.* The consultant must determine to what degree the data should be shared with the client and when these data should be shared. In sharing a great deal of data, it is possible to overload the client or to create undue fear and anxiety in an early stage of the helping process. On the other hand, it is only through exposure to the data that the client can develop an understanding of the change effort and the motivation to become involved in it.

Orientation Toward Collaboration

Identifying the real client(s) and deciding how to relate to him, her, or them are often two of the most difficult tasks facing the consultant. Frequently a consultant relates too exclusively to the top executive or the initiator of the contract, when, in order to be effective, he or she should relate to a total staff unit or some other population as the client system. Consequently, the intervention decision may have the wrong focus.

    Often the consultant must deal with the important and puzzling issue of how to relate to one or more insiders as part of an ad hoc change-agent team, without creating difficulties with the rest of the system because of this special working relationship. Another dilemma involves deciding to what degree to be an expert and an advocate of certain goals, procedures, and methods and to what degree to be a nondirective facilitator and supporter of the client system's mobilization of its own resources and goals.

Risk Taking

Even though a client expects new experiences and activities as a result of working with a consultant, this prospect usually generates caution or insecurity about departing from the tried and true. Consequently, the consultant is almost always faced with a series of questions about the appropriate degree of risk taking. The problem becomes how to reduce the client's stress and defensiveness and still introduce enough change to make a difference. A continuing dilemma is balancing interventions that stimulate significant change effort with those that support the client system as it participates in problem-solving activities to modify functioning and its environment.

Orientation Toward Resource Identification and Use

At some point with almost every client, a consultant must answer the following questions:

- Can I offer what the client needs now or later?
- Are other resources also needed?
- Will the client be disappointed if I clarify areas of inadequacy in my competencies and resources?
- How do I feel about suggesting that other sources of help are needed to complement me or to replace me?

We believe that all consultants need practice in facing these questions and working through the answers with their clients.

Decisions About Interventions, Context, and Timing

Consultants tend to become so focused on questions of what to do and say in their interactions with clients that they forget other intervention decisions concerning the context, the timing, and the methodology of offering help. We believe it is important for the consultant to deal with these four issues:

1. **Direct or Indirect Intervention.** The consultant should consider whether the intervention should be direct and face-to-face or performed through some other medium. Over the years in our consultation practice, we have discovered an increasing variety of situations in which the use of written memoranda and telephone calls seems superior to the greater time and energy expended in face-to-face interaction. The writing

of a memorandum to a client can organize and clarify ideas, and the reading of it allows the client to do some thinking and reacting before a face-to-face session. An exchange of memos often is a very effective preliminary preparation for a conference. Using the telephone to make queries or to offer support has great advantages, particularly after a face-to-face relationship has been established. The consultant may have a face-to-face relationship with one person or with a small number of key people who serve as links to the total client system. This saves the time, energy, and money required to have a direct relationship with all parts of the system.

2. *Focal Point of the Intervention.* When determining the focus of an intervention, the consultant must choose one of these possibilities:

- An individual in his or her intrapersonal dynamics;
- Interpersonal relationships and cliques, subgroups, or clusters within the client system; or
- The total system or organization.

Redl (1941) developed a principle in working with teachers that also applies to the consultant's situation: One should not intervene to influence an individual member of the group unless the effect is at least neutral, if not positive, for the total group; similarly, one should not intervene to influence the total group unless the impact will be at least neutral, if not positive, for each individual in the group. In determining the focal point of the intervention, therefore, the consultant must consider the potential side effects.

3. *Whether to Intervene.* Part of our work with consultants involves practice in making decisions concerning interventions. In one of the most interesting activities that we use, each consultant records those points in an interaction in which he or she is tempted to intervene but decides against doing so. A review of these decisions usually indicates that some of them were lost opportunities, passed by because of a lack of ability to generate alternatives and to choose among them. But it seems clear that at other times the consultant involved was wise to say and do nothing, having sensed that an intervention might inhibit the client's work, might be timed poorly because of the client's lack of readiness, or might complete work that the client would prefer to initiate later if given the time.

We believe that the deliberate decision not to intervene is an important part of intervention decision making; it should be sharply differentiated from the consultant's neglect or avoidance of decisions that he or she is not able or ready to make.

4. *Proactive or Reactive.* One of the most critical decision dilemmas in working with client systems is the degree to which the consultant should be a proactive initiator of interventions or a responder to the problem-solving efforts and initiatives of the client. There is a broad range of practice between (1) the relatively nondirective responder and supportive encourager of the client's activities and (2) the enthusiastic advocate and active initiator of interpretations, methods, and activities. It is our belief that all consultants must clarify for themselves the values and styles that they use in this area of decision making.

An Example of the Decision-Making Process

In order to provide a sense of what we believe is involved in the intervention decision-making process, we have selected one of Ron's decision analyses to share. This is the kind of analysis we have done many times as part of our growth and development as consultants.

The Situation

The administrator of a community outreach unit asked Ron to help to resolve a conflict between the outreach unit and a volunteer-services team regarding duplication of services to clients. The outreach unit was headed by a clinical psychologist, and the volunteer-services team was headed by a social worker.

The Decision Dilemma

Ron had to decide whether to regard the administrator who contacted him as the client and work out a contract with him or to regard the clinical psychologist and the social worker or the organizations themselves as clients.

Decision/Action Alternatives

Ron's alternatives for action were as follows:

- He could accept the request as legitimate.
- He could ask the administrator to involve all members of the two organizations and solicit their acceptance of his role as helper.
- He could tell the administrator that he needed to meet with both the clinical psychologist and the social worker to determine whether they could accept a client relationship with him.
- He could ask the administrator to convene all relevant parties to meet with him to explore their readiness and the possibility of their becoming his clients.

Value Criteria That Were Considered

The following value criteria were considered in this situation:

- The administrator had the right and responsibility to intervene to improve the quality of service rendered by his staff.
- Ron did not believe that it was ethical to try to influence the decisions and behaviors of people who had not accepted his right to try to help them.
- Ron believed that a large proportion of those who need help do not accept this need or feel able to ask for help, so "selling them" on his ability to help was appropriate.
- The administrator was probably a crucial part of the entire system of services; therefore, if a significant solution was to be found and maintained, the administrator had to be included in the intervention.
- Ron thought that he was an appropriate resource for this type of problem.

The Final Decisions and Actions

Ron decided on the following course of action:

- He told the administrator that he was challenged by the problem and thought there was a good chance that he could help.
- He also stated that he could not agree to work on the problem unless the clinical psychologist and the social worker—and perhaps the other members of both organizations—agreed to his involvement.
- He agreed that the administrator might have difficulty achieving cooperation without coercion or avoiding the creation of counterdependent resistance. Therefore, he suggested that he should take some responsibility for "selling" his service, if the administrator would sanction his contacting the clinical psychologist and the social worker.
- He stated that if he could develop both people's readiness to work with him, he would expect a meeting with the administrator, the clinical psychologist, and the social worker to arrive at a mutual agreement on his role, his time, his access to the two organizations, and so forth. He clarified that the clinical psychologist and the social worker would be the clients.

Value Principles That Were Used

Ron used the following values in making his final decision regarding a course of action:

- The working contract with the client should be mutually voluntary or should become voluntary early in the process.
- The definition of "client" should include those who need to be influenced to achieve the desired outcome and to maintain it.

Skills That Were Used

In this particular case, Ron used the following skills:

- Communicating his value rationale to the administrator in such a way that the administrator did not feel threatened, accepted the rationale, and accepted the idea that Ron knew what to do and how to do it;

• Meeting with the heads of the two organizations to support open communication about the problem and to elicit their readiness to work on it; and

• Projecting the kind of work that would be needed and obtaining support and sanction for working with both staffs involved.

QUALITY ASSURANCE

One of the most exciting challenges for a consultant is to establish the support relations and situations that ensure continuing growth in the quality of his or her performance. Some of our efforts in this respect are discussed in the following paragraphs.

Shared Debriefing

After consultations or training sessions, most consultants experience a strong temptation to abandon the situation for a while. However, we find that it is best to debrief what happened immediately. This process takes only thirty minutes or so and is extremely important to the consulting effort. When we meet for such a debriefing, the conversation progresses roughly in this way:

Ron: I had the feeling that there was a lot of "foot dragging" during that session and that some hidden agendas were operating. Did you feel that way?

Gordon: Yes, I did. Was it something we said, or was it connected with some norms they have about risk taking?

Ron: I thought once of legitimizing ambivalence as a normal thing in this situation and asking them to share their feelings.

Gordon: I doubt if they were ready. What if we. . .?

Often part of debriefing is brainstorming about alternative ways to address what happened during the session.

Critical-Episode Role Play

The consultant may ask several peers to join him or her in a two-minute role play of an intervention situation. One of the peers plays the client; the consultant plays himself or herself; and the remaining peers observe the interaction. The role play is stopped at a critical point that requires the consultant to respond. The following is an illustration of this kind of role play and the ensuing discussion between colleagues:

Consultant to School Principal: I'm glad I was able to get away today. Is there something I could help you with?

Principal: I hope so. Mr. Diamond, the third-grade teacher, and Miss Rush, the fifth-grade teacher, both seem to be having trouble with discipline. Could you confer with them and see what needs to be done?

At this point the role play is stopped. Each colleague observer makes notes about all the things that he or she can think of to say or do, chooses the intervention that seems most appropriate, and writes a paragraph about why it seems most appropriate. The observers then share their decisions and rationales, and the consultant who requested their participation summarizes the ideas presented and what he or she might do. Subsequently, the consultant tries the chosen intervention in a continuation of the role play and receives feedback from his or her colleagues. Some groups of consultants use tapes of actual conversations with clients when they hold feedback sessions of this type.

Triad Skill Practice

One of our designs involving practice, feedback, and further practice starts with a group of consultants who brainstorm intervention dilemmas that call for the use of particular consultation skills. Each consultant selects one dilemma and the corresponding skill on which he or she would like to work and forms a group with two other consultants who have also chosen dilemmas and skills. Within each triad one member takes a turn playing the role of consultant in the chosen dilemma, practicing the associated skill; another triad member plays the role of client, and the third member observes and makes notes about his or her observations. At the conclusion of the interchange, the consultant's handling of the situation is debriefed, with both of the other two members providing feedback. Subsequently, the same role-play situation is rehearsed several times, with the client and observer exchanging roles, so that the consultant can practice the skill that he or she has selected; after each practice the consultant's handling of the situation is debriefed. This procedure is repeated until each member of each triad has practiced several times.

There is no substitute for this kind of behavioral practice. Consultants cannot develop necessary skills merely by talking about them.

Feedback from Clients

One available and typically unused resource for improving interventions is feedback from clients. We find that asking clients for their reactions wins their appreciation and their respect. In addition, the consultant who requests feedback from a client models one important element of an effective two-way relationship, thereby increasing the client's openness and readiness to learn.

The following are some typical questions included on questionnaires that we ask our clients to complete:

- The most helpful thing you did today was _____.
- The thing you did (or did not do) that I found least helpful was _____.
- Something I learned from our work today is _____.
- What you did to facilitate this learning was _____.
- Words or phrases I would use to describe your consulting today are _____."

Resisting Temptation

At the beginning of a new client relationship, it is sometimes tempting to reuse a design or activity that worked well in an intervention with another client. This temptation is a trap. Our belief is that each client's situation represents a new challenge and opportunity. Only after thoroughly diagnosing a client's special needs can a decision be made to *adapt* a design or activity that has been used before.

Balancing Internal and External Cues

Converting diagnostic decisions into action and design decisions is a point at which much of the quality of consulting performance is revealed. One's previous experience with interventions and their consequences is the repertoire of inner resources that one uses to interpret and use the diagnostic data from each new client. The proper blending of new data and past experience is the basis for creative, high-quality decision making during interventions.

REFLECTIONS ON THIS CHAPTER

Gordon: I think one of the toughest challenges of consulting is looking at each client as a new opportunity rather than as "like that client we worked with last year." It's very easy to fall into that trap.

Ron: When I have a tempting accumulation of similar data from several clients, I know there are numerous relevant design and intervention tools that could be used with any or all of these clients. I avoid looking into these tools until I've completed the initial diagnostic data collection with the new client. Then the uniqueness of the new client's problems and situation are clear enough to push toward appropriate modifications of past interventions.

Gordon: Another challenge in making intervention decisions is to think simultaneously about individual, group, and organizational dynamics. Trying to do this really stretches my abilities.

Ron: In my consulting efforts, I find it easiest to neglect individual differences or organizational culture. But if I start with a group focus and stretch my thinking to encompass individual and organizational concerns, some unexpected alternatives for intervention usually emerge. Some of these insights come from reading the new contributions of our professional colleagues.

Gordon: Yes. What you're talking about is the greatest challenge of all: to create the personal support conditions necessary for continuing to grow and learn as a consultant.

REFERENCES

Redl, F. (1941). *Diagnosing teacher training needs.* Unpublished manuscript.

Rosenberg, P.P. (1951). *An experimental analysis of psychodrama.* Unpublished doctoral dissertation, Harvard University.

4

Consultant Roles

When helping an individual, a group, an organization, or a larger social system, a consultant fulfills a number of roles that he or she judges to be appropriate for the client, the situation, and his or her own style. Argyris (1970) and Blake and Mouton (1976) clarify consultant roles in terms of the intervention strategies used. The intervention decisions are steered by the values and sensitivities of the consultant and the needs of the client. Bennis (1973) identifies three roles for a change agent: training, consulting, and applied research. Although Bennis does not focus solely on consulting, he emphasizes the roles of educator and fact finder.

In their monograph, Lawrence and Lorsch (1969) propose a three-fold role for an OD specialist: educator, diagnostician, and consultant. They write:[2]

> If an OD specialist is going to be effective at achieving both commitment to, and more sophisticated solutions for, organization development issues, he will have to clearly view his role as that of an educator and a diagnostician, as well as a consultant. That is, he will have to be able to develop techniques for identifying organization problems and analyzing their causes. He will have to be able to educate managers and other organization members in the use of concepts to conduct diagnoses and to plan action. Finally, he will have to act as a consultant in providing his own action proposals for the managers to consider.

Menzel (1975) and Havelock (1973) add a fourth role of linker to the three indicated above. They present the linker function as the awareness of resources and the linking of the needs of the client and relevant resources.

---

[2]From *Developing Organizations: Diagnosis and Action* (p. 95) by P.R. Lawrence and J.D. Lorsch, 1969, Reading, Massachusetts: Addison-Wesley. Reprinted by permission of the publisher.

In the provocative article, "Consultants and Detectives," Steele (1969) suggests that consultant roles are similar to those of fictional British detectives. Both roles share several attributes, as follows:[3]

- The temporary nature of involvement in a system;
- The focus on gathering evidence and trying to solve the puzzles which it represents;
- The potential for "dramatics";
- The potential action orientation and the excitement it contains;
- The stance of "expert" in behavioral science; and
- The stimulation of working on several "cases" at once.

Steele points out several responsibilities that must be assumed by the consultant to prevent the aforementioned satisfactions from getting out of hand:[4]

- Promoting consciousness of self;
- Avoiding incorporation into the client system;
- Arranging for some collaborator or "sounding board" with whom to check perceptions, ideas, and feelings;
- Using intuition as one means of generating ways to understand the situation; and
- Being wary of the tendency to lump people into the oversimplified categories of "good" and "bad."

These varied observations make it difficult to define one set of specific roles for a consultant. In a helpful model, Margulies and Raia (1972) divide consultative roles into "task-oriented" and "process-oriented" roles. Their concept is indicated in Figure 3.

As a result of our own experience and search, we have developed a descriptive model that presents the consultant's role along a directive and nondirective continuum. Behavior varies in its degree of directiveness. In the more directive consultant role, the consultant assumes leadership and directs the activity. In the nondirective mode, the consultant provides data, for the client to use or not, as a guide for the

---

[3]Reproduced by special permission from *The Journal of Applied Behavioral Science.* "Consultants and Detectives," by Fred I. Steele, Vol. 5, No. 2, p. 200. Copyright 1969 NTL Institute for Applied Behavioral Science.

[4]"Consultants and Detectives," p. 200. Reproduced by special permission from *The Journal of Applied Behavioral Science.*

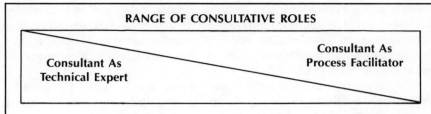

RANGE OF CONSULTATIVE ROLES

Consultant As
Technical Expert

Consultant As
Process Facilitator

Task Orientation

Process Orientation

ROLE CHARACTERISTICS

Task	Process
1. *Problem Verification:* by "expert" evaluation and collection of data.	1. *Problem Verification:* by "problem sensing" and facilitating a clear articulation that includes attitudes and feelings.
2. *Problem Solving:* provides ideas and opinions, designs research for data, and develops solution for the client-system.	2. *Problem Solving:* works on the problem-solving capability of the system, improves problem-solving process, and facilitates creativity.
3. *Feedback:* presents research data with "expert" interpretations.	3. *Feedback:* provides meaningful data, facilitates assimilation of data, and allows for client interpretation.
4. *Utilization of Research:* makes specific and concrete recommendations based on data.	4. *Utilization of Research:* develops client use of data and facilitates action by client based on learning.
5. *Relationship to Client:* is objective, detached, and task oriented. Connection is short term and problem oriented.	5. *Relationship to Client:* is personal, involved, and process oriented. Connection is long term and system oriented.
6. *Involvement:* is primarily with the problem to be solved.	6. *Involvement:* is primarily with people and groups in the organization.
7. *Systems Approach:* concern is with implications of the problem for other parts of the organization.	7. *Systems Approach:* concern is for collaborative relationships and exchange of resources among parts of the organization.

Figure 3. Task-Oriented and Process-Oriented Roles

client's self-initiated problem solving. These roles are not mutually exclusive but may manifest themselves in many ways at any stage in a particular client situation. We see these roles as spheres of competence rather than as a static continuum of isolated behavior. The model is presented in Figure 4.

In the past the consultant role has been used in a nondirective mode, particularly by those in the clergy or counseling field, or as an expert function by engineers and other technical specialists who are called in by clients to solve problems. Both of these functions, as well as others, are proper and legitimate when performed appropriately by a competent internal or external consultant.

ROLE DESCRIPTIONS

Advocate

When the word *advocate* is mentioned in the context of consulting, several descriptions come to mind. The consultant as an advocate may be seen as:

- A fighter;
- A strong believer;
- A provocateur;
- One who is aggressive in attempting to influence others;
- A person with convictions and values;
- A person with guts;
- A persuader; and
- An expert with a highly directive posture.

These descriptions evoke a strong image. The consultant as an advocate is seen as using power, influence, and an element of mobilizing force or a threat of consequences to impose his or her ideas and values. The dictionary confirms at least part of this image:

ad·vo·cate, one who defends, vindicates, or espouses a cause by argument; a persuader

If the consultant is viewed in general as a person who attempts to help others solve problems, the advocate role can present some difficulties. It would seem that an advocate might make a practice of telling people what to do. However, research into the nature of the helping

MULTIPLE ROLES OF THE CONSULTANT

Objective Observer	Process Counselor	Fact Finder	Identifier of Alternatives and Linker to Resources	Joint Problem Solver	Trainer/ Educator	Information Specialist	Advocate

CLIENT

CONSULTANT

LEVEL OF CONSULTANT ACTIVITY IN PROBLEM SOLVING

Nondirective							Directive
Raises questions for reflection	Observes problem-solving process and raises issues mirroring feedback	Gathers data and stimulates thinking	Identifies alternatives and resources for client and helps assess consequences	Offers alternatives and participates in decisions	Trains client	Regards, links, and provides policy or practice decisions	Proposes guidelines, persuades, or directs in the problem-solving process

Figure 4. Directive and Nondirective Roles

relationship suggests that dependence on the helper is usually not in the long-range interests of the client; clients must have an active role in the solution of their own problems. Because many consultants may not think it helpful, or even possible, to function without promoting their personal values, a dilemma exists. The consultant has values and wants to be of influence, but mere push is usually not helpful to the client.

One method of sorting out this situation is to make a distinction between the content and the process advocate:

- In the *content* or positional advocacy role, the consultant influences the client to choose or accept particular goals, values, or actions.
- In the *process* or methodological advocacy role, the consultant influences the client to become active as a problem solver and to use certain methods of problem solving—but is careful not to become an advocate for any particular solution.

The consultant who is a content advocate attempts a conscious influence on choice of goals and means. For example, a content advocate might actively promote producing brown widgets rather than red widgets, or choosing computer systems over manual systems, or choosing particular curricular materials.

The consultant who is a process advocate attempts a conscious influence on the methodology underlying the client's problem-solving behavior. For example, a process advocate might suggest an open meeting rather than a closed one in order to increase trust in the system. In this sense the advocate consultant is less concerned with what is specifically said at the meeting than with the general method or approach to the meeting itself. Both of these views of the advocate involve the values of the consultant, and both assume that the consultant will intervene in some way that exerts pressure on the system. However, the scope of the goals or values is quite different. The goals of the content advocate are rather specific, but those of the process advocate are broad and more flexible.

A consultant often becomes an advocate of content or process, or of both to some degree. The type of advocacy role that the consultant assumes is contingent on several factors, such as the consultant's personal goals, a minimal receptivity on the part of the client, and the interpersonal versus technical nature of the task. The consultant considers the time frame, the risks, and alternative consequences. Although there may be more potential risk to external advocates, they are also less "owned" by client systems and, consequently, can usually exert more influence on these systems.

In a sense it is not possible for a consultant to avoid being some type of advocate. By the consultant's very presence, he or she has influence on the client. The question becomes more a decision about what the consultant will advocate and how he or she will carry out this advocacy. For consultants who see themselves in a helping relationship with their clients, process advocacy becomes an overall feature of their approach.

In summary, the choice of advocate behavior is derived from the consultant's values and beliefs about the appropriate content and style of influence and their consequences.

Information Specialist

Another role is that of the information specialist who, through his or her knowledge, skill, and professional experience, is engaged as an internal or external consultant to provide special-knowledge services. The client is mainly responsible for defining the problem and the objectives of the consultation, and the consultant assumes a directive role until the client is comfortable with the particular approach recommended. In some cases consultants never move out of this role, as indicated by Steele (1969):[5]

> I think the role of "expert" is a quite seductive one for the consultant—all the more so in behavioral science since the variables and their relationships are often quite fuzzy and complex. It can be quite personally gratifying to have others see me as someone who really "knows" what is going on or what should be done in a given situation. Besides personal gratification on the part of the consultant, another factor pushes him toward the stance of expert: the client's wish to see himself safely in the hands of an expert who is wise and able so that the anxiety over present or future difficulties can be reduced.

Although the needs of both the consultant and the client may encourage this role of expert, the consultant should not follow this behavior pattern exclusively. The issue of increased client dependence is not the only potential difficulty associated with the role of exclusive expert; it also may lead to poor problem solving because of limited consideration of alternatives.

------

[5]Reproduced by special permission from *The Journal of Applied Behavioral Science.* "Consultants and Detectives," by Fred I. Steele, Vol. 5, No. 2, pp. 193-194. Copyright 1969 NTL Institute for Applied Behavioral Science.

Some consultants feel that the role of process specialist is appropriate, but that the role of content expert should be avoided. This position is espoused by Schein (1969), who states that:[6]

> [the] consultant should not withhold his expertise on matters of the learning process itself; but he should be very careful not to confuse being an expert on how to help an organization to learn with being an expert on the actual management problems which the organization is trying to solve.

We believe that there may be times when giving advice on both methodology and solutions is appropriate. However, the use of the advocacy role must be selective and restrained. Everyone likes to give advice, but such advice is resisted if it is not offered at a particular time in the relationship, situation, and problem-solving process. Frequently the consultant gives information early to help meet the immediate needs of the client. Later in the relationship, the consultant may act as a catalyst and procedural helper in implementing the recommendations that have been made.

Trainer/Educator

Consulting about innovations may require training and education within the client system. The consultant may be a creator of learning experiences or a direct teacher, using the skills of a designer, leader, and evaluator of the learning process.

We believe that every internal and external consultant should be able to function in this role. The capacity to train and educate is essential to many helping situations, particularly when a specific learning process is indicated in order for the client system to acquire competence in certain areas. For example, we have observed that the implementation of new organizational methods, such as management by objectives (MBO) or strategic planning, often fails because the consultant and the organization's leaders do not give proper attention to the training process. If people in the organization are not skilled in one-to-one relationships, interviewing, and on-the-job observation, the procedures and forms of an innovation will not work.

---

[6]From *Process Consultation: Its Role in Organization Development* (p. 120) by E.H. Schein, 1969, Reading, Massachusetts: Addison-Wesley. Reprinted by permission of the publisher.

The consultant might consider some form of training function as part of the helping role when:

- An organization wants to develop its own strategy for employee self-development and self-confidence and encourage authentic interpersonal competence in its staff;
- A commitment has been made to re-educate staff members in human relations in order to alter their attitudes and behavior;
- An organization wants to develop or cultivate the interpersonal skills of key individuals to increase the effectiveness of individual and group problem solving;
- An organization wants to promote an adaptive style of interpersonal competence, focusing on the value and development of responsibility, esteem, and self-acceptance; or
- A client system needs to develop new job skills or enrich current jobs for better performance.

When functioning as a trainer/educator, the consultant must be able to:

- Assess the training needs related to the problem involved;
- Develop and state measurable objectives for learning experiences;
- Understand the learning and change process;
- Design a learning experience;
- Plan and design educational events;
- Go beyond traditional training and use heuristic laboratory methods;
- Employ multiple learning stimuli, including various kinds of media;
- Serve as a group teacher or trainer; and
- Help others learn how to learn.

The role of trainer/educator may be part of a continuing consulting relationship. For example, one of us, in consulting with the president of a community college about his desire to develop a five-year plan for the college, served as an expert and joint planner. After this phase of consultation, the consultant suggested an organizational-renewal conference. Subsequently, a weekend conference was planned and attended by the consultant, the president, ten administrators, ten students, ten trustees, and ten faculty members.

During the last two sessions of the conference, which were designed for action planning and implementing, the group made fourteen recommendations for action. The president indicated that one fell in his area of responsibility; in addition, two were referred to the trustees, one to the student council, one to the faculty senate, and one to the director of admissions. To address the eight remaining recommendations, the president and the group set up eight task forces. The task force of shortest duration lasted for three months and the longest for fourteen months. Within fifteen months all fourteen recommendations had been acted on by the appointed person or group.

This experience increased the participants' involvement, identified problem areas, and set in motion actions that led to the adoption of a five-year plan. Training in joint problem solving became a natural, flowing part of a two-year consultation process.

Joint Problem Solver

The role of helper in problem solving involves collaborating with the client in all of the perceptual, cognitive, emotional, and action processes needed to solve a problem. While a problem is being clarified, the consultant helps to maintain objectivity while stimulating ideas and interpretations. In addition, the consultant can help to isolate and define the basic factors that cause a problem and perpetuate it, or that could be activated to solve it. The consultant usually assists in weighing alternatives, sorting out the most critical causal relationships that may affect alternative solutions, and developing a course of action. In this role the consultant is involved in analysis and decision making as a peer. However, when helping to resolve problems involving conflict, the consultant also may assume the role of third-party mediator.

Under the right circumstances, a consultant in this role brings to a client and to a situation important resources through the ability to:

- Perceive the situation accurately;
- Provide a wider perspective of the situation by testing assumptions;
- Define goals clearly;
- Express and test alternatives;
- Provide a sense of reality;
- Confront sensitive areas;
- Save client time and resources;
- Reinforce commitments;
- Link existing resources to other resources;

- Catalyze action;
- Divide the problem into manageable parts; and
- Use and expand client resources.

These contributions clearly require receptivity on the part of the client and flexibility on the part of the consultant.

Identifier of Alternatives and Linker to Resources

In this role the consultant identifies alternative solutions to a problem; establishes criteria for evaluating each alternative, determining its cause-and-effect relationships; assesses the probable consequences of each alternative; and links the client with internal and/or external resources that may be able to provide additional help in solving the problem. However, the consultant does not participate in the decision-making process when the final solution is selected.

Some people feel that the role of linker is separate from that of identifier. According to Havelock (1973), the linker is "someone who knows about resources, knows about people's needs, and knows how to bring client and resources together" (p.18). However, we believe that linking should be a part of the process of identifying alternatives, so that action is not limited by the resources of the client or the consultant. The good consultant does not limit the alternatives and resources to his or her own area of expertise. As French and Bell (1973) point out:[7]

> In the future, organization development specialists must know much more about such matters (i.e., the task, technical and structural aspects and their interdependencies) and must establish linkages with practitioners in such fields as management science, personnel and industrial psychology, operations research, and industrial engineering in order to provide a broader range of options for organizational intervention.

---

[7]From *Organization Development: Behavioral Science Interventions for Organization Improvement* (p. 195) by W.L. French and C.H. Bell, Jr., 1973, Englewood Cliffs, New Jersey: Prentice-Hall. Reprinted by permission of the publisher.

Fact Finder

In this role the consultant functions basically as a researcher. Fact finding is an integral part of the consulting process, whether it be for developing a data base or for diagnosing intricate client problems. It is one of the most critical aspects of problem solving, and it is often the one that receives the least attention. This function includes developing criteria and guidelines to be used in collecting, analyzing, and synthesizing data. The process of collecting can be accomplished through an approach as simple as listening or one as complex as a formal, computer-scored survey. The consultant should have at his or her command a number of such approaches.

The internal consultant may be able to collect relevant data more readily than the external consultant. The external consultant may not have such easy access to data, but may have the advantage of credible objectivity. In either case, any of five primary methods can be employed to gather data:

- Interviewing (either on a one-to-one basis or in group situations);
- Administering a questionnaire;
- Observing;
- Analyzing records and documents; and
- Administering and analyzing appropriate tests.

The consultant must know how and when to employ each technique and must secure the collaboration of the client. Some important questions to answer when choosing a data-collection method include the following:

- Which method will provide the most timely data?
- Which method will cost the least in terms of both monetary and human resources?
- Which method best fits the client's current needs?
- Which method is most consistent with the client's values?

The collection of data, by whatever method, is an integral part of the consultant's job. A consultant must realize that using any technique affects the functioning of the client system to some degree, and he or she must know how much direct intervention the system can tolerate. An ethical helper must take care to respect confidences and to protect the sources of information.

Fact finding provides the consultant with a valuable understanding of the client's processes and performance in meeting goals, schedules, and objectives. From these insights the consultant and the client can evaluate how well a change process is working and how well it has met or is meeting its problem-solving objectives.

In addition, the way in which the consultant works with the client to plan and implement the data-collection process serves as a model to the client system. Therefore, the consultant must know what data to look for, where to find them, how to secure them in the least disruptive manner, and how to motivate the client to become interested in the findings. The skill of planning and giving data feedback is an essential part of the fact-finding role.

Process Counselor

It is essential that the consultant function as a process specialist. Schein (1969) defines this role as follows:[8]

> Process consultation is a set of activities on the part of the consultant which help the client to better perceive, understand, and act upon process events which occur in the client's environment.

The most significant aspect of this definition is the implication of a diagnosis conducted jointly by the consultant and the client, the intention being that the consultant will transfer to the client the skills necessary to continue such diagnosis.

The consultant's major focus is on the interpersonal and intergroup dynamics affecting the problem-solving process. Frequently, process consultation is closely allied with fact-finding activities through the use of observation. The process consultant directly observes people in action and conducts interviews with management personnel from the president down; the purpose is to obtain facts and report the data to the client system in order to improve organizational relationships and processes. The process consultant must be able to effectively diagnose who and what is hindering organizational effectiveness and to report these observations to the appropriate person or persons in the organization.

---

[8]From *Process Consultation: Its Role in Organization Development* (p. 9) by E.H. Schein, 1969, Reading, Massachusetts: Addison-Wesley. Reprinted by permission of the publisher.

The consultant works with the client to develop the client's diagnostic skills in addressing specific problems, focusing on *how things are done* rather than what tests are performed. He or she helps the client to integrate interpersonal and group skills and events with task-oriented activities and to support the improvement of relationships.

Objective Observer

The role of objective observer consists of a series of consultant activities directed at stimulating the client toward some insights into growth, a discovery of more effective methods, a look at long-range change, and greater independence. This is the most nondirective of the consulting roles. The consultant communicates no personal beliefs or ideas to the client and is not responsible for the work or the outcome. Instead, the client is solely responsible for whatever direction is chosen.

Part of the function of the objective observer is to ask questions that help the client to clarify and confront the problem involved and to make decisions. The consultant may also paraphrase, probe, and be empathic, experiencing with the client the blocks that initially provoked the problem. In this role the consultant acts as a philosopher, taking a long-range view.

The behaviors required of the objective observer are similar to those of the process counselor, but some of the emphasis is different. An interesting issue to explore is the relationship between consultant roles and client decisions. Typically, the consultant activities at both extremes of the role spectrum do not terminate until a decision has been reached—by the consultant in the case of the advocate, and by the client in the case of the objective observer.

The role of objective observer requires some trade-offs that should be considered when using this approach. One trade-off involves, on one side, the consultant's commitment of time and flexibility, and on the other side, the client's acceptance and trust of the consultant.

Two additional points can be made about the nondirective observer role:

1. When performing as an objective observer, the consultant must continue the role until the client reaches a decision. This somewhat reduces the consultant's degree of control over the time spent with the client.

2. This form of consultation tends to increase the levels of frustration within the client system. Although this heightened level of frustration usually precedes increased self-awareness on the part of the client, it may be unacceptable to a business organization or to an executive in a demanding environment.

This role, like all the others, is usually not carried out in a pure form; most consultants use multiple roles in working with a client.

CRITERIA FOR CONSULTANT ROLE SELECTION

In this section we examine the variables that determine the consultant's choice of role for a particular client situation and phase of the consulting relationship. We have made it clear that (1) there are numerous consultant roles that can be interpreted in many ways, and (2) the role assumed by the consultant may vary from moment to moment. To speak of roles as separate and distinct is a distortion of reality. Therefore, it is more realistic to consider which role is predominant at any given moment or for the longest period of time.

One might ask, "To what degree does a consultant make a conscious decision about the role that he or she will assume?" We believe that the consultant reacts to a situation with his or her whole being and with behavior that is determined less by a process of deliberate decision making than by a complex of trained reactions and experiential responses, some of which are unexplainable. But in the process of learning consultation, reflection about such distinctions and decisions is important.

Our criteria for role choice are more descriptive than prescriptive, resulting from what we have seen and felt. We have found no way to measure with confidence which factors are key determinants in the consultant's role selection. More often than not, the literature on the subject describes personal experience and attempts to relate that experience to universal constants. The following factors are not the only ones that can be used as criteria, but we believe them to be among the most important and the most common in practice.

The Nature of the Contract

The mutual understanding between the consultant and the client system concerning their professional relationship is their contract. Sometimes this understanding takes the form of a written document, and sometimes it is simply an oral agreement. In either case it becomes a *psychological contract.* Difficulty in coping with the contract can arise from the endless variations of it that can exist in the minds of involved individuals.

Because change is inherent in the nature of human relationships and because the presence of a new force (the consultant) changes the very nature of the problem to be addressed, the contract also must change and evolve to varying degrees. Its first form, which is established either during the consultant's entry or before it, probably sets the initial hierarchy of consultant roles. The contract changes with each development that follows, but the way in which it changes is largely determined by its initial form. If the initial contract is structured and specific, the consultant's roles may remain relatively unchanging (barring a new contract). However, if the initial contract is general and unstructured, the consultant's roles may vary continually.

Goals

The formulation of goals also can be seen as a process. Not only do the consultant and the members of the client system begin with multiple goals, but they change them and reorder their priorities from time to time. Again, as the presence of the consultant affects the perceptions and operations of the client system, it also has impact on the goals of that system.

A third-party role is relevant for a consultant who is involved with resolving an intergroup conflict. But if the two groups are to assume responsibility, the role of trainer/educator would be relevant for helping them to develop conflict-resolution skills.

Norms and Standards of the Client System and the Consultant

By norms and standards, we mean the full spectrum of values from etiquette to morals and life style. Unlike the consulting contract, norms and standards resist change. Although they, too, are processes, they tend to change more slowly as the client system ages. In fact, one of the frequent unheralded tasks of the consultant—particularly the process consultant—is to change the client's value systems.

Generally, the narrower the norms and standards of the client system, the more constricted the role of the consultant. This is true as long as (1) the norms and standards tend to be consistent from one member of the client system to the next, and (2) the consultant does not choose the tactic of changing the client system by confronting it with an unexpected role.

To the degree that the norms and standards of the client system and those of the consultant differ, the consultant functions more toward the directive end of the directive-nondirective scale. Under these conditions the consultant may use other role orientations to support that of the advocate in trying to secure congruence with the client.

Personal Limitations and Inclinations of the Consultant

We believe that the determining factors in the consultant's choice of roles are his or her natural predilections and competencies. Personal style, as Walton (1969) points out, strongly conditions the roles and interventions of the consultant. Interpersonal competence, including self-awareness, is the first skill that Beckhard (1969) lists as a requirement for the OD consultant. Self-awareness that leads to interpersonal competence implies an acceptance of one's limitations. Therefore, role choice is likely to be affected by the consultant's view of the role in which he or she feels most effective and comfortable. The greater the versatility and the broader the role repertoire of the consultant, the more likely he or she is to succeed in a variety of settings.

What Worked Before

All people are victims of *set*—that proclivity of the mind to reuse what has worked before. Consultants are no exceptions. As long as the nature of the client system tends to remain the same from one consulting assignment to the next, it is likely that the consultant will use the same roles. But to be able to deal with varied client systems, the consultant should be able to recognize this tendency toward set and adapt to changing contexts.

Internal and External

It is our feeling that a consultant's role choice tends to be related to the degree that he or she is an integral member of the client system. For example, the consultant who is subordinate to the same supervisor as the group that he or she is working with frequently is forced into the role of police officer or watchdog. This is less likely to be true for someone from another part of the organization. Of course, we know of many exceptions to this rule, but it is more often true than not.

Role expectations for internal consultants are limited insofar as they are not independent agents and their functions within organizations are specified. In addition to encountering resentment for intervening, the internal consultant must face preconceived notions of how much he or she will tell the supervisor and what specific changes will be effected.

Because of these circumstances, the internal consultant usually follows one of two trends. One is to become more external in functioning (for example, as the result of a company's decision to make its consulting staff an independent concern). The other trend is to become more constrained in assuming roles and spheres of operation.

Events

Events external to the consultation process can have a profound impact on the client system and/or the consultant and can cause the consultant to change his or her role. The birth of a child, the beginning of a war, a change in organizational leadership, race riots, or fluctuations in the stock market can change the complexion of the client system or the outlook of the consultant to the point that a change in roles occurs.

Earlier in this chapter, we presented a model that linked role selection with degrees of directive and nondirective behavior. That model, like all others attempting to depict human situations, has limited utility and validity; it is true and accurate part of the time. We ask the reader to see role selection as a process determined by a number of other processes and factors, some of which have been described. As in any system of interrelated processes, the selection of one role causes changes in the determining processes themselves, which in turn modify the role selection, and so on. Because of the complexity of this situation, we have been unable to construct a model for it. But if the behavior of the consultant is perceived as a process within a process, then the realities of consultation in action have been communicated.

REFERENCES

Argyris, C. (1970). *Intervention theory and method: A behavioral science view.* Reading, MA: Addison-Wesley.

Beckhard, R. (1969). *Organization development.* Reading, MA: Addison-Wesley.

Bennis, W.G. (1973). Theory and method in applying behavioral science to planned organizational change. In A. Bartlett & T. Kayser (Eds.), *Changing organizational behavior* (pp. 73-75). Englewood Cliffs, NJ: Prentice-Hall.

Blake, R.R., & Mouton, J.S. (1976). *Consultation.* Reading, MA: Addison-Wesley.

French, W.L., & Bell, C.H., Jr. (1973). *Organization development: Behavioral science interventions for organization improvement.* Englewood Cliffs, NJ: Prentice-Hall.

Havelock, R.G. (1973). *The change agents' guide to innovation in education.* Englewood Cliffs, NJ: Educational Technology Publications.

Lawrence, P.R., & Lorsch, J.D. (1969). *Developing organizations: Diagnosis and action.* Reading, MA: Addison-Wesley.

Margulies, N., & Raia, A. (1972). *Organization development: Values, process, and technology.* New York: McGraw-Hill.

Menzel, R.K. (1975). A taxonomy of change-agent skills. *Journal of European Training, 4*(5), 287-288.

Schein, E.A. (1969). *Process consultation: Its role in organization development.* Reading, MA: Addison-Wesley.

Steele, F.I. (1969). Consultants and detectives. *Journal of Applied Behavioral Science, 5*(2), 193-194, 200.

Walton, R.E. (1969). *Interpersonal peacemaking: Confrontations and third-party consultation.* Reading, MA: Addison-Wesley.

5

Ethical Dilemmas and Value Guidelines[9]

Achieving personal and group guidelines and commitments for ethical behavior is crucial to the competence of a consultant. In this chapter we examine the ethics of giving help, look at selected ethical dilemmas, and present some guidelines for behaving ethically as a consultant.

We want to develop awareness of the complexity of several ethical dilemmas. These dilemmas include the intrusion of preconceived images of the consultant-client relationship, dangers in the manipulation of human behavior, and the issue of achieving congruence between values and behavior.

In any area of helping, the consultant occupies a position of trust; therefore, the ethical aspects of his or her work and relationships occupy a significant place in the discussion of the consulting process. The work of any professional helper requires the constant exercise of discretion and judgment. The client may not be qualified to appraise the quality of service being offered or the risks involved and, therefore, may have to rely for support and protection on the consultant's standards of conduct. The client is justified in expecting high standards and can derive confidence from knowing that a code of professional consulting behavior exists.

Shay (1965) views ethics as:[10]

> . . . standards of professional conduct and practice which stem from the nature of the profession. They are consistent with the profession's purposes and functions in society and are generally considered to be the best ways of applying the knowledge and skills peculiar to it.

---

[9]We acknowledge Paul R. Holland and Jane Schmithorst for their help in our search of the literature on professional ethics.

[10]From "Ethics and Professional Practices in Management Consulting" by P.W. Shay, 1965, *Advancement Management Journal, 30*(1), p. 13.

According to Shay, ethics represent the attitudes, principles, and approaches that:[11]

- Contribute to the success of the professional's special work;
- Make for equitable and satisfactory client relationships; and
- Relate his profession properly to the part of society which it serves.

THE PROFESSIONAL

In discussing professional codes and ethics, we should note what is generally meant by the term *profession*. The Association of Consulting Management Engineers (1966) defines it as:[12]

> an occupation requiring extensive preliminary intellectual training, pursued by others and not merely one's self, and accepting as the measure of achievement one's contribution to society rather than individual financial reward.

All of the standard definitions of professions include elements of dedication, of giving one's ethical positions a place of extreme importance, of taking pride in applying one's knowledge and skills, and of functioning with integrity. In a field as complex and varied as consulting, ethical practice implies far more than simply profiting from the mistakes of the profession. It demands a willingness to be alert to novel situations and to respond to them as they develop.

Shay (1965) defines the characteristics of a professional in any profession as:[13]

- Knowledge of the profession, its philosophy, principles, and practices;
- A continuing discipline of study and responsibility for assisting in the advancement and dissemination of professional knowledge;
- A standard of conduct governing the relationships of the practitioners with prospective clients, clients, colleagues, members of allied professions, and the public;

---

[11]"Ethics and Professional Practices in Management Consulting, " p. 13.

[12]From *Ethics and Professional Conduct in Management Consulting* (p. 4) by Association of Consulting Management Engineers, Inc., 1966, New York: Author.

[13]"Ethics and Professional Practices in Management Consulting," p. 14.

- A motive of service, as distinguished from primary preoccupation with making profit; and
- Professional pride—the belief on the part of the practitioner in the worthiness of his/her calling, and the influence this conviction has on guiding his/her actions.

Therefore, the basic postures that allow a person to function effectively in a professional role are the following:

- Acquiring the knowledge and learning the disciplines of the profession;
- Learning to apply professional knowledge and skills effectively;
- Always putting client interests ahead of one's own interests or those of the group to which one belongs;
- Maintaining high standards for serving clients; and
- Behaving at all times with a professional bearing.

These postures establish the basic responsibility of developing and using ethical guidelines for decision making and behavior in any consulting relationship and role.

We believe that readers who are interested in being effective helpers, but who do not think of themselves as members of a particular profession, will find it helpful to think of their efforts as "professionalizing" themselves as helpers.

SOURCES OF ETHICAL GUIDELINES

People who have had little experience in consulting may wonder why it is not a simple matter to conduct all professional dealings in accordance with the highest ethical standards. The difference between the proper and the improper should be clear enough. But it is not that simple. All too frequently the consultant faces decisions that involve ethical questions not easily resolved. Some consultants may find themselves working in areas in which ethical standards are vague and ambiguous. It is also the case that in many instances the consultant must walk a decision-making tightrope, trying to balance fairly the sometimes conflicting interests of all those with whom he or she is professionally associated.

As a professional practitioner, the consultant is a maker of value judgments. Consulting involves activities in which choices must be made between alternative courses of action. When choosing between possible alternatives, a consultant is making a choice between two or more values; and making such a choice often involves an ethical decision.

The consultant makes some value judgments in a social context for which the larger society has already determined the most appropriate value choices. These "dos and don'ts" are enshrined in legal codes of prescriptions and prohibitions. Consequently, the guidelines for consulting decisions and behavior are sometimes found either in law or institutional procedures.

This level of consulting guidelines is what philosophers call *normative ethics*. A particular behavior is good or right if it is consistent with the accepted norm. As long as the consultant is content to accept the given norm, he or she can make value decisions with relative ease. "He is culture bound and happy in its claims" (Golightly, 1971).

The process of making value judgments becomes painful when the consultant is no longer content with the provision of existing law and institutional guidelines or when the issues are not covered by precedents and norms. It is difficult for a consultant to know that a given idea, recommendation, or policy is right or that a proposed change is better unless he or she knows what "right" and "good" mean.

Statements of value differ from statements of fact, and values cannot be verified in the same way as facts. Values arise from human beliefs and desires. People establish goals or end values and experiment with means to achieve their goals, creating a continuum of ends and means that are subjected to norms about appropriate behaviors. These norms are continually tested in the experiential world. When the norms work, people keep them; when they do not work, people are motivated to revise or discard them. Taking a rigid, moralistic stance toward values often short-circuits the circular process whereby the consequences of one's actions lead to a re-examination of beliefs and motives.

According to Fletcher (1968), there are basically only three alternative routes or approaches to follow in making ethical decisions: (1) the legalistic, (2) the lawless or unprincipled, and (3) the situational. With the legalistic approach, one enters into every decision-making situation with a whole code of preformulated rules and regulations. The lawless approach consists of entering into a decision-making situation with no principles or maxims whatsoever, except perhaps self-interest. The situational approach lies between these two. Since every situation is unique, one must rely on the situation itself, then and there, to provide clues for the creation of an ethical decision. With this approach one enters into every consulting situation with the ethical maxims developed previously as a result of experiencing somewhat similar situations.

Central to the use of ethical guidelines in most consulting situations is an awareness that circumstances alter cases. The person using situational ethics is willing to make full and respectful use of principles, treating them as maxims but not as laws. There is no real quarrel here between situational ethics and an ethics of principles, unless the principles become hardened into laws or regulations.

Ethics deals with human relations, and situational ethics is concerned with people rather than codes. A common objection to situational ethics is that it calls for more self-discipline in commitment to values than most people are able to muster.

The multiple pressures and rapid changes that have characterized the era following World War II have increased the frequency and intensity of the value dilemmas of society. This increased conflict among values contributes to a general attitude of questioning traditional values, a trend that appears to be a characteristic of the postindustrial society. Values change through a process of challenge and accommodation between the system of existing values on the one hand and technologies, action pressures, and reluctant social changes on the other.

Consistent with these conflicting social influences has been the dual emergence of an individualistic ethic and a social ethic. The individualistic ethic glorifies the freedom of the individual, competition between one person and another, and self-determination as the value goal of life. The social ethic emphasizes the importance of the individual's responsibility to the group and to the society at large; it is based on the assumption that the interactive social system provides the primary way of meeting human needs. Golembiewski (1965) says that neither of these ethics by itself is adequate: "Both are morally unspecific; and neither. . .can muster evidence to show it is necessary and sufficient for inducing effective performance under existing conditions" (pp. 45-47).

Three more specific ethical or value systems have been emerging that are relevant for consideration by consultants. These are the scientific ethic, the humanistic ethic, and scientific humanism. Each of these orientations has come increasingly to the fore in the last two decades in response to major social changes. Scientific values tend to emphasize rationality, moderation, flexibility, calculation, planning, and prudence as guidelines. Humanistic values stress freedom, spontaneity, creativity, participation, and self-actualization. Scientific humanism is proposed as an integration of these two frameworks.

Probably the most important indications of the application of the scientific ethic are the new science-based analysis and decision-making techniques that are increasingly prevalent in business and government.

These techniques, such as operations research and system analysis, call for clarity in the specifications of goals and, therefore, serve to make value preferences explicit. As evidence of the humanistic ethic, the humanistic trend in psychology developed by Maslow (1965) is probably most forceful and relevant to the interpersonal aspects of the consulting process. Maslow emphasized openness of communication, mutuality of decision making, personal growth, and fulfillment.

CODES OF ETHICS

An ethical code for a profession helps to ensure fair treatment for clients and provides for the protection of their rights. We believe that the consultant should act in accordance with these ethical principles:

- Follow guidelines set by historical reference regarding behavior that is attractive and justifiable to the client;
- Inspire the client's faith that he or she will behave in a way that is beneficial to the client; and
- Signify that he or she is committed to doing a good job in the client's interest in return for the client's trust and confidence.

In every profession it has been necessary to establish a code of ethics to protect the interests of clients. Such a code represents an effort to record some of the more definable rules of conduct. Furthermore, it signifies the voluntary assumption of the obligation of self-discipline above and beyond the requirements of law.

A code that attempts to deal fully with the ethical dimensions of the professional's role in society can serve a useful function. It is educational, providing members of the profession with guidelines for the kind of ethical behavior that, according to the historic experience of the group, is most likely to justify the confidence of the client. In addition, a code can narrow the area in which a professional has to struggle with uncertainty.

A number of professional organizations have developed codes of ethics for their members. In the following paragraphs we briefly examine those of the Association of Consulting Management Engineers, the American Society for Training and Development, and the Academy of Management. Then we present our own code of ethics, drawing on these and on our own experience.

Code of the Association of Consulting Management Engineers

The Association of Consulting Management Engineers (1966) has outlined the purposes of a code of professional ethics as follows:

- It helps the practitioner to determine the propriety of his or her conduct in professional relationships;
- It indicates the kind of professional posture that the practitioner must develop and maintain if he or she is to succeed;
- It gives clients and potential clients a basis for confidence that the professional sincerely desires to serve them well and places service ahead of financial reward; and
- It gives clients a basis for confidence that the professional will do his or her work in conformity with professional standards of competence, objectivity, and integrity.

Code of the American Society for Training and Development

The American Society for Training and Development (1977) has published its Code of Ethics. From this code we have chosen the following items as particularly relevant to the best interests of a consultant-client relationship. Consultants shall:[14]

1. Not conduct activities that may cause any colleague or training participant unnecessary embarrassment or disparagement;
2. Not violate confidences or break promises, unless disclosure of confidential information serves professional purposes or is required by law;
3. Limit their activities as facilitators of change to functions for which they have been adequately trained and shall abstain particularly from areas of psychological activity for which they have no professional qualification;

---

[14]From "Code of Ethics" (p. 30) by American Society for Training and Development, in *Who's Who in Training and Development,* 1977, Washington, DC: Author. Reproduced by special permission from the American Society for Training and Development. Copyright, 1977.

4. Not knowingly distort or misrepresent facts concerning training and development activities to any individual, organization, or employer;

5. Openly share information and data that will advance the state of the professional art;

6. Maintain a professional attitude toward the introduction of new knowledge in the field of training and development;

7. Recognize the desire of individuals and organizations to improve themselves and permit no exploitation of this desire by unethical use of the profession or its members; and

8. Recognize that society in general accords status to consultants and in return they have an obligation to serve the needs of society.

The first three items relate to and uphold the aspect of the profession that encourages the validation of openness and trust between members of the client system and the consultant. Items four through six concern ethical responsibility and are designed to protect and support the growth of the profession. Item seven protects the rights of both clients and the profession. The eighth item relates to the responsibility and obligation of the profession toward society in general: The profession should be able to recognize and justify the effect that its practices have on society at large.

Code of the Academy of Management

The Academy of Management, Division on Organization Development (1976), has adopted a code of ethics, from which we have chosen the following relevant items. Consultants shall:[15]

1. Place the needs of the client organization above their own and not let their own needs interfere in the consulting process;

2. Respect the integrity and protect the welfare and interests of client organizations;

3. Fully inform client organizations of aspects of the potential relationship that might affect the client's decision to enter the relationship; and

4. Not misrepresent their own professional qualifications, affiliations, and purposes, or those of the organizations with which they are associated.

---

[15]From "Proposed Code of Ethics" by Academy of Management, Winter 1976, *Organization Development Division Newsletter,* pp. 1-2. Reprinted by permission of the publisher.

The first three items deal generally with the obligation of any professional in dealing with a client and, more specifically, with the OD consulting relationship. The purposes of the last item are to serve the well-being of the client and to uphold the profession's good name.

The Authors' Code

Borrowing from the codes of ethics previously discussed and from our own experience, we have developed the following code.

CODE OF ETHICS FOR THE PROFESSIONAL CONSULTANT

1. Responsibility

The consultant:

- Places high value on objectivity and integrity and maintains the highest standards of service; and
- Plans work in a way that minimizes the possibility that findings will be misleading.

2. Competence

The consultant:

- Maintains high standards of professional competence as a responsibility to the public and to the profession;
- Recognizes the boundaries of his or her competence and does not offer services that fail to meet professional standards;
- Assists clients in obtaining professional help for aspects of the projects that fall outside the boundaries of his or her own competence; and
- Refrains from undertaking any activity in which his or her personal problems are likely to result in inferior professional service or harm to the client.

3. Moral and Legal Standards

The consultant shows sensible regard for the social codes and moral expectations of the community in which he or she works.

4. Misrepresentation

The consultant avoids misrepresentations of his or her professional qualifications, affiliations, and purposes and those of the organization with which he or she is associated.

5. Confidentiality

The consultant:

- Reveals information received in confidence only to the appropriate authorities;
- Maintains confidentiality of professional communications about individuals;
- Informs the client of the limits of confidentiality; and
- Maintains confidentiality in preservation and disposition of records.

6. Client Welfare

The consultant:

- Defines the nature of his or her loyalties and responsibilities in possible conflicts of interest, such as between the client and the consultant's employer, and keeps all concerned parties informed of these commitments;
- Attempts to terminate a consulting relationship when it is reasonably clear that the client is not benefiting from it; and
- Continues being responsible for the welfare of the client, in cases involving referral, until the responsibility is assumed by the professional to whom the client is referred or until the relationship with the client has been terminated by mutual agreement.

7. Announcement of Services

The consultant adheres to professional standards rather than solely economic rewards in making known his or her availability for professional services.

8. Intraprofessional and Interprofessional Relations

The consultant acts with integrity toward colleagues in consultation and in other professions.

9. Remuneration

The consultant ensures that the financial arrangements for his or her professional services are in accordance with professional standards that safeguard the best interests of the client and the profession.

10. Responsibility Toward Organization

The consultant respects the rights and reputation of the organization with which he or she is associated.

11. Promotional Activities

The consultant, when associated with the development or promotion of products offered for commercial sale, ensures that the products are presented in a factual way.

THE USE OF CODES OF ETHICS

The adoption of a code of ethics, no matter how complete and detailed, is not enough. Members of a profession should study the code, know the reasons for its provisions, and understand its general importance.

Simply establishing a code does not guarantee a change in the ways in which members of a profession function. Regardless of how good a code may be, it is ineffective unless accompanied by some practical system of enforcement that is accepted by practicing professionals. A number of professional associations in the consulting field have developed well-defined procedures for handling alleged violations of their codes. Some of the most clear-cut sanctions have been developed and publicized by the American Psychological Association (APA). In 1953 the APA developed a code to guide the psychological profession in the earlier stages of its development. After its experience in applying the code, the APA revised it in 1959, 1963, and again in 1966.

The Committee on Scientific and Professional Ethics and Conduct (CSPEC) was established as an instrument by which members of the APA could judge their peers concerning alleged violations of the code. Although many potential infractions have been called to the attention of the CSPEC, the committee has not found it necessary to confront the alleged offender in every instance. Sometimes the documentation provided by complainants is inadequate, or the behavior described as unethical is not necessarily so. Many situations are resolved constructively through correspondence about the circumstances surrounding the behavior or activities in question. American Psychological Association members who are found guilty of unethical behavior, as measured against the code, are expelled from the association or placed on probation.

The APA and its members are also concerned with the professional conduct of people who purport to be psychologists but do not belong to the association. In the case of a nonmember, however, disciplinary action can be taken only by the government or other agencies that have jurisdiction over the person involved. The CSPEC (1968) deals only with questions of ethics, and then only in an investigatory and advisory role. Disciplinary action is the responsibility of the board of directors of the APA, which takes into account the findings of the committee.

The APA has used the findings rendered by CSPEC as an index of the serviceability and fairness of its code. It also has compiled a casebook containing disguised material drawn from the findings of the committee and has cited the principles involved and the conclusions reached. The Casebook on Ethical Standards of Psychologists (American Psychological Association, 1967) furnished precedents for the APA and for local ethics committees, and it is also used for educational purposes by psychologists in general. Thus, for the APA, the code and the casebook are important from both a judicial and an educational standpoint.

One other development in the enforcement of ethical behavior is the requirement in some states that consultants be licensed, a requirement already in effect for many psychologists. We endorse this licensing procedure; furthermore, we believe that flagrant violations of the APA code should result in the revoking of the license of the consultant who is responsible for this behavior. Such potent sanctions would surely enforce the code as the accepted law of professional behavior.

Codes usually are addressed to the correction of known deficiencies and incidents of malpractice experienced in the past. However, codes falter in dealing with the unforeseeable or dimly envisioned future; they can only suggest a principle of decision making. When a complicated or previously unrecorded situation occurs, the consultant must stand alone in his or her decision making (Beck, 1971).

The most important aspect of formulating a code is the acceptance of a basic norm of morality that will properly sustain the code and indicate practical applications in situations too specific to be covered by the code. Effectiveness in application, of course, depends on the competence of the consultant.

Many groups besides the specialists' professional societies are defining and using competency-based criteria for membership. Such groups include the Institute of Management Consultants, the International Association of Applied Social Scientists, NTL Institute for Applied Behavioral Science, Association for Creative Change, Society of Professional Management Consultants, Organization Renewal, and the International Consultants Foundation.

ILLUSTRATIVE ETHICAL DILEMMAS IN CONSULTING

We see several ethical dilemmas that offer present or potential challenges in the consulting process. Although both the consultant and the client bring into the consulting process their expectations of the relationship, these expectations are not always in agreement and, therefore, can present dilemmas. Three factors involved in these kinds of dilemmas are as follows:

- The client's expectations regarding the nature of help needed and how it should be acquired;
- The intrusion of ethical standards acquired by the consultant in his or her other professional experiences; and
- Conflicts that arise between the ethics identified with the consultant's nonprofessional life and the value judgments that are peculiar to a consultation process.

The integrity of the consultant can be challenged when demands from the client push the limits of the consultant's ethical concepts and guidelines. The manner in which such a problem is handled is both a professional and an ethical consideration for the consultant. For example, the client may want a particular answer or method that the consultant, for professional and ethical reasons, refrains from offering. Such a professional and ethical judgment requires the ultimate in flexibility on the part of the consultant in order to accomplish an effective relationship and to achieve the client's goals. The client's expectations as well as those of the consultant must be accommodated.

A consultant often must function not only as a helper but also as a social scientist, an engineer, or an educator. This overlap in roles makes complete role segregation difficult, and ethical problems arise in the consultant's attempts to integrate his or her professional orientation as a consultant with that of another role. The consultant may find that the norms introduced from professional consulting associations are threatened by the demands of client behavior and the here-and-now consulting situation. Consequently, a conflict develops between the ethical demands of the two roles.

Because they are less systematically articulated by the consultant, nonprofessional aspects of the consultant's values present a less definable ethical problem. However, the norms of the consultant's nonprofessional life do present dilemmas, such as the issue of whether it is ethical to engage with a client system whose purpose and goals are opposed to the consultant's personal, religious, or political beliefs. Should a consultant who is a conscientious objector, for example, become engaged in consultation for a national defense project? Should a consultant who favors strict gun control consult with the National Rifle Association?

These alliances would be ethical only if the consultant's relationship with the client system were completely divorced from the consultant's personal beliefs and the client were made aware of the consultant's values. These circumstances are not likely, and a consultant would be justified in declining such an assignment because of a conflict of personal norms. This is an ethical problem because its resolution involves the future of the consultant's personal beliefs and nonprofessional associations as well as the effectiveness and integrity of the consultation process.

The consultant must personally resolve these ethical conflicts. In such situations we have found it helpful to seek guidance from respected associates who can offer constructive advice based on their experience and insights.

In addition, these potential dilemmas should receive attention in the preservice and inservice training of consultants. There should be opportunities for training in making choices, not toward standard solutions but rather toward solutions that are right for the individual consultant and for the client.

THE MANIPULATION DILEMMA

The recognition that consulting usually involves, directly or indirectly, the deliberate influencing of human attitudes, values, and behavior creates a variety of ethical ambiguities. The product of the consultant's work may meet the immediate needs of the client, yet its long-range consequences and its effect on other units of the client system may be problematic. It is necessary, therefore, that the consultant be concerned with the larger impact of the processes and outcome to which he or she contributes. One way to deal with the dilemma of influencing others' personal and social destinies is to explain the "voluntary nature of the change relationship" (Lippitt, Watson, & Westley, 1958) to the client and to ensure that the client understands and accepts it.

Kelman (1965) discusses in depth this same ethical dilemma for the social scientist/consultant, whose work has a manipulative nature. The basic dilemma has two dimensions. To those who hold the enhancement of freedom of choice as a fundamental value, any deliberate influencing of the behavior of others constitutes a violation of their basic humanity. On the other hand, effective behavioral change involves the change agent's use of power and control as well as the potential imposition of the change agent's values on the client system. According to Kelman:[16]

> The two horns of the dilemma, then, are represented by the view that any manipulation of human behavior inherently violates a fundamental value, but that there exists no formula for so structuring an effective change situation that such manipulation is totally absent.

Kelman cites two dangers that consultants face in influencing the client toward change:[17]

> One is the failure to recognize that [the consultant] is engaged in the control of the client's behavior. The other is intoxication with the goodness of what he is doing for and to the client, which in turn leads to a failure to recognize the ambiguity of the control that he exercises.

The consultant must recognize these dangers in order to take steps to control them.

Kelman suggests three steps to mitigate the manipulation involved in a change agent's efforts:

- Increasing one's own and others' awareness of the manipulative aspects of a change agent's work and the ethical ambiguities inherent therein, by clarifying one's own values to oneself and the client and by allowing the client to respond;
- Deliberately building protection against or resistance to manipulating the process, by minimizing one's own values and by maximizing the client's values as the dominant criteria for change; and

---

[16]From "Manipulation of Human Behavior: An Ethical Dilemma for the Social Scientist" by Herbert C. Kelman, 1965, *Journal of Social Issues, 21*(2), p. 33. Reprinted by permission.

[17]"Manipulation of Human Behavior: An Ethical Dilemma for the Social Scientist," p. 37. Reprinted by permission.

- Setting the enhancement of freedom of choice as a central goal for one's practice, by using professional skills and relationships to increase the client's ability to choose and the range of choices.

Benne (1959) describes an internal conflict arising from the different interests of the consultant's "scientist self" and "consultant self." As Benne says, the conflict may take the form "of anxiety that one is losing his scientific hard-headedness in enjoying the psychic rewards of helping one's client" (p.64). Benne suggests that the consultant may reduce personal dilemmas, anxieties, and uneasiness by giving careful thought to the formulation and articulation of his or her civic, religious, and personal philosophies and moralities—a precondition for adequately recognizing and handling ethical issues.

This ethical dilemma is similar to the one discussed earlier that concerns the consultant's selection of clients. Factors to consider in resolving either of these dilemmas may include the needs of the client system, the needs of the consultant, potential learning for the consultant, the consultant's personal attraction to a client, and the potential contribution made to society by dealing with a particular client.

ETHICAL DILEMMAS OF INTERNAL OR EXTERNAL CONSULTANTS

Guidelines for the ethical behavior of an internal consultant differ somewhat from those for an external consultant. The major difference can be attributed to the objectivity, or lack of it, with which a consultant might behave.

Collier (1962) says that the way in which one looks at a business depends on where one happens to be. It makes a big difference whether one is on the outside looking in or on the inside looking out. A member of an organization can never quite see the organization in the same way as a nonmember. Certain responsibilities, loyalties, hopes, and fears inevitably color and enrich a member's perceptions of the organization and lead to a different frame of reference from that of the outsider looking in.

In 1969 the American Management Association conducted a twenty-month study of the internal-consultant process used by approximately sixty commercial firms (Dekom, 1969). The results were as follows:

1. *Consulting-Staff Characteristics.* Staff members were generally well educated, analytical, perceptive, diplomatic, broadly experienced,

and temperamentally suited to a staff role. In addition, they were held to high personal and professional standards of conduct. However, these staffs also were depleted through promotions of good people to operating positions.

2. **Staff Training and Development.** Objective training was received outside the company, but each company furnished its consultants with a handbook on professional behavior.

3. **Compensation.** The amount of money earned was not dependent on the success of the individual consulting project.

4. **Source of the Assignment.** Most assignments originated with requests from a client-subsidiary or a subordinate-level manager.

5. **Launching the Assignment.** An assignment usually was launched by a letter providing an overview of the scope of the work. Subsequently, the project objective was outlined by the client; then the consultant spelled out the probable involvement of client personnel and did an estimate of on-the-job and elapsed times, fees, and out-of-pocket expenses.

6. **Reports.** Both oral and written reports of plans of action were made to the client. When a report was written, the client reviewed a draft before finalization and voiced any significant objections to the consultant, who then accommodated these objections in the final report.

In most cases the consultant reported only to the client. Relations with the client were treated as confidential; findings and recommendations were not reported to higher management without the client's permission.

7. **Implementation.** The consultant assisted in implementation. The effectiveness of the consultation was measured in terms of action taken by the client and repeat requests for help.

8. **Fees.** Cases in which consultants charged clients directly were more effective than those in which the cost was charged to a firm's overhead.

9. **Use of Public Consultants.** Internal consultants advised on the use of outside help when there was a peak demand for trained personnel, when unusual expertise was needed, or when the appearance as well as the fact of complete objectivity were necessary.

From the experience of the firms contacted in this research, it can be concluded that, except for the reduced objectivity with which the internal consultant is handicapped, there was little difference between the ethical guidelines for internal consultants and those for external consultants. In addition, from our discussions with both internal and external helpers, we feel that the ethical standards and concerns in consultation are relevant to one and all.

Examples from Our Experiences

Ron: As I review the various efforts to arrive at value guidelines for the "shoulds" of appropriate professional behavior, I keep having the same uneasy feelings I have about using lectures as a way of changing behavior. The "shoulds" are supposed to be values guiding behavior; but we don't get much guidance about how the shoulds might operate as components in specific intervention decisions, and we don't get many clues about how to internalize guidelines and make them operational so that they actually influence our behavior along with the other forces that influence our decisions.

Gordon: I think you're right. Maybe that's why we get the emphasis on the peer-system policy compliance rather than a focus on learning how to use these norms in actual decision making.

Ron: Let me try an example to see if it helps us get down to the way values could and should play a role in making decisions. In a recent situation, the major value issue for me as a consultant was a very basic one: whether, when, and how to advocate to my client certain beliefs I hold about proper values and behaviors for people in the client system.

The Situation

The client board was in the process of setting two-year goals that I felt were too ambitious (that is, not feasible for accomplishment in that period). The members of the board also were neglecting to examine the probable duplication of services with interdependent agencies, which potentially could have had some very harmful results in terms of neglected clients and wasted funds.

The Decision Dilemma

Should I tell the board members what goals I believed were reasonable and advocate collaborative interaction with the other agencies, or would I be abdicating my consultant role if I told them what they ought to do?

My Decision/Action Alternatives

1. I could present my recommendations by being an advocate for my position (my beliefs).
2. I could present my ideas as another alternative for the board members to consider.
3. I could recommend problem-solving procedures that I thought would help them discover alternatives and consequences.

4. I could help them work on the goals that they had chosen, no matter how I felt about these goals.

5. I could decide that their values were incompatible with mine and that I should withdraw from helping.

Value Criteria That I Considered

1. Every client has the right and responsibility to make his or her value decisions (that is, to decide on goals).

2. The consultant has the responsibility for helping the client to use problem-solving methods and resources that are as appropriate as possible in making such decisions and plans.

3. The consultant should accept the fact that value differences are normal; the client should not be expected to share the consultant's values.

4. If I feel that my clients' behavior is going to be harmful to themselves or others, I may need to mobilize resources beyond my own to prevent damage.

My Decisions and Actions

1. I proposed two steps in goal setting. The first was to brainstorm all possible, desirable outcomes or goal images. The second was to engage in a priority-setting exercise that included feasibility testing by projecting the action steps required to realize the two-year goal images.

2. I added my own items as part of the brainstorming process.

3. I role played other agency directors, reacting to the board members' goal ideas, and recommended collecting data from the other directors as part of the final goal-setting process.

4. When there was a complaint about "paying too much attention" to how other agencies would be affected by the goal decisions and plans, I raised questions about motivation and value issues.

5. I decided to continue as a consultant in spite of several decisions with which I disagreed.

Value Principles That I Used

1. There is a basic difference between positional advocacy and methodological advocacy (that is, between telling the board members what I thought they should believe or do and advising them regarding problem-solving methods that I believed they should use).

2. The development and use of values and skills constitute a process of several steps. (Expecting the board members to be "perfect" or to function the way I thought they should at any given point in our relationship would have been unrealistic and would have precluded my being helpful in this process.)

3. The consultant has the responsibility for sharing his or her own perspectives as a resource, but in the context of mutual problem solving rather

than in the context of creating client dependence or displaying expert status.

4. The consultant may need to terminate the contract if he or she feels that the collaboration has become a basic violation of ethical values and that the client is unwilling or unable to work on these issues.

Skills That I Used

I used all of the following skills during this particular consultation. Each is part of the discipline of becoming an effective professional helper; each requires practice with feedback, debriefing, and further practice.

1. Making a credible presentation of the value of brainstorming alternatives and testing consequences;
2. Leading the client group in these activities;
3. Role playing those who are not present without creating defensiveness; and
4. Sharing personal beliefs without attributing undue weight to them during problem solving.

Gordon: I find this a very helpful analysis. What it illustrates is that value criteria are just some of the factors to be considered in any intervention decision and that behavioral skills are crucial in determining whether the values can actually be incorporated into that decision. It also helps me to see how probably every intervention decision we make involves considering multiple value criteria rather than simply following the guidelines of one particular value.

Ron: This matter of multiple values or guiding principles has always seemed to me to be very crucial if we are to take our values seriously. I think the most important guiding values in my professional life have been the guidelines of methodological values formulated by Ken Benne, which he believes are derived from a basic analysis of democratic principles and of the principles of applied scientific method.

SEVEN METHODOLOGICAL VALUES TO GUIDE INTERVENTIONS

Benne (1959) puts forth these seven values to guide consulting interventions:

1. ***Experimentation.*** The processes of giving help should be experimental, aimed at developing more adequate ways of thinking about values and of handling a partly unknown future. The provisional plans

that are made should include a commitment to continuing evaluation and revision in the light of feedback on the consequences of the experiments.

2. *Two-Way Interaction and Influence.* A consultant will be influential with a client to the degree that the client perceives himself or herself as able to influence the consultant.

3. *Objective Confrontation of Tasks and Situations.* Appropriate interventions are based on objectivity rather than on maintaining or augmenting the prestige or status needs and systems of the client or the consultant. In other words a consultant must ignore such categories as "expert," "experienced," "very young," and "in charge."

4. *Emphasis on Client Learning.* Helping should include objectives and techniques for supporting a process whereby the client learns, learns how to learn, and/or relearns. This implies that one of the criteria of effective consultation is the increased capacity of the client to cope with problem situations in the future without the collaboration of the consultant.

5. *Use of All Available Resources.* Appropriate procedures of helping include efforts to search for and make full use of available, relevant information and experience. This value is in opposition to the notion that the consultant is the major resource; instead, one of the consultant's responsibilities is to serve as a link to other resources.

6. *Voluntary Assumption of Responsibility.* An appropriate attitude toward helping is to regard all client units as parts of interdependent systems in which there is a voluntary assumption of responsibility to give and take and to solve problems through mutual processes of growth and development. This attitude is the opposite of the view that the major objectives of the helping process are individual adjustment and personal independence.

7. *Self-Evaluation, Self-Correction, and Self-Renewal.* Appropriate helping processes must incorporate procedures whereby both the consultant and the client can accomplish self-evaluation, self-correction, and self-renewal. This value includes the notion of openness to the revision of values and goals as well as techniques and means.

If consultants make these values operational in their professional lives, most of the ethical norms discussed earlier in this chapter will be respected and will be evident in consultations. The big challenge is not to create bigger and better lists of ethical norms, but rather to put these values to work in a practical sense.

REFERENCES

Academy of Management. (1976, Winter). Proposed code of ethics. *Organization Development Division Newsletter.*

American Psychological Association. (1967). *Casebook on ethical standards of psychologists.* Washington, DC: Author.

American Society for Training and Development. (1975, November). Code of ethics. *Who's Who in Training and Development,* p. 30.

Association of Consulting Management Engineers. (1966). *Ethics and professional conduct in management consulting.* New York: Author.

Beck, C.E. (1971, December). Ethical practice: Foundations and emerging issues. *Personnel and Guidance Journal,* p. 321.

Benne, K.D. (1959). Some ethical problems in group and organizational consultation. *Journal of Social Issues, 15*(2), 60-67.

Collier, A.T. (1962). *Management, man, and values.* New York: Harper & Row.

Committee on Scientific and Professional Ethics and Conduct. (1968). Rules and procedures. *American Psychologist, 23*(5), 362-366.

Dekom, A.K. (1969). *The internal consultant* (Research study 101). New York: AMACOM.

Fletcher, J. (1968). *The situation ethics debate.* Philadelphia: The Westminister Press.

Golembiewski, R.T. (1965). *Men, management and morality: Toward a new organizational ethic.* New York: McGraw-Hill.

Golightly, C.L. (1971, December). A philosopher's view of values and ethics. *Personnel and Guidance Journal,* p. 289.

Kelman, H.C. (1965). Manipulation of human behavior: An ethical dilemma for the social scientist. *Journal of Social Issues, 21*(2), 31-46.

Lippitt, R., Watson, I., & Westley, B. (1958). *The dynamics of planned change: A comparative study of principles and techniques.* New York: Harcourt Brace Jovanovich.

Maslow, A.H. (1965). *Eupsychian management.* Homewood, IL: Richard D. Irwin.

Shay, P.W. (1965). Ethics and professional practices in management consulting. *Advanced Management Journal, 30*(1), 13-20.

6

Designing Participative Learning

Our observation is that the designing of learning sessions is one of the most neglected areas of professional practice, and it is one of the most important. Much time is wasted in "playing it by ear" or in assuming that "an emergent design" will be sensitive to the client's needs. Instead, to use training time effectively the consultant must prepare carefully by putting himself or herself in the client's shoes and reflecting carefully on data about the client's needs. We believe that systematic planning of any necessary learning session is an ethical responsibility of every professional helper. Developing a good design for participative learning facilitates the client's readiness and flexibility with regard to changing plans when new needs emerge. We use the following ten assumptions as guides in designing learning sessions:

1. Every client group should be perceived and approached as different from any preceding group.

2. In every client group there are differences in readiness, experience, skill, and motivation with regard to participating in learning activities.

3. The client learners should be influential in planning the design for the learning activities (for example, by providing needs and interests data or by selecting representatives to help in the planning process).

4. To facilitate this participative influence, the consultant should model the building of resources needed to take initiative in the planning process.

5. It is important that the consultant build a two-way feedback process and provide evidence that the feedback is being used.

6. The consultant should identify and legitimize the influence (leadership) network existing within the client group.

7. The design should include plans for supportive follow-up.

8. The consultant should form teams of peers in the client group to support learning and follow-up.

9. One of the purposes of all designing is to pass on methodological skills to client learners so that they can become professionally independent of the consultant's guidance and support.

10. At all levels of the client system—individual, group, and total organization—one of the consultant's major challenges is to link information to relevant applications, to an intention to act, to goal setting and action planning, to skill development in such areas as presenting actions plans to management, and to risk taking in appropriate situations.

CLIENT EXPECTATIONS ABOUT THE LEARNING PROCESS

Assumption number 10 in the previous discussion refers to the consultant's responsibility in helping to meet the expectations of learners in client systems, whose proactive influence is an increasingly widespread phenomenon. The consumer revolution of the Sixties, Seventies, and Eighties has spread to the learning situation and the helping relationship. Trainees, like students in various kinds of educational institutions, have discovered that they have the right and the power to influence how their needs and interests will be defined, what they will be taught, and how they will be taught. Many teachers and facilitators of "required" learning activities have recognized the increasing tendency of participants to assert their needs and to resist or avoid directive teaching efforts, and consultants are seeing the same trend.

Norman Cousins (1981) summarizes this consumer revolution beautifully:[18]

People today want a larger share in the decision making about their lives. However, much as they may have respect for the superior learning of their

---

[18]From *Human Options* (p. 37) by N. Cousins, 1981, New York: W.W. Norton & Company, Inc. Reprinted by permission.

teachers, they believe they themselves have something of value to offer in the determination of what it is they should be taught and even how they are to be taught. They see themselves not just as receptacles for instruction, but essential participants in the educational experience. They mirror the central tendency of this age—which is the quest for individual respect. Finally, they shun those for whom thinking is reflexive, rather than reflective, and increasingly subject to computerized decisions.

Also, the sponsors of educational, training, and consultative efforts are making increasing accountability demands. They are seeking various kinds of "hard" evidence of accountability in terms of concepts and skills learned and used by learners to improve their productivity, competence, and commitment.

MEETING CLIENT EXPECTATIONS THROUGH THE LINKAGE MODEL

One way for the consultant to meet client expectations about learning is through the use of what we refer to as the *linkage model*. This model is based on a series of crucial linkages that the consultant helps the client to establish in order to learn and to act in accordance with learning. These nine linkages are described in the following paragraphs.

Linkage 1: Input of Information

There are a number of different learning resources: research findings, demonstrations of practice, case studies, experiences of others, nonverbal communication, documentary movies, and so forth. In most cases the client learner is unaware of these resources until the consultant—by providing input, stimulating inquiry, and modeling the motivation to learn—links the client with them. As a result of this linkage effort, the client acquires information.

Linkage 2: From Information to Understanding

The challenge of the consultant is to help the client learner to process this information into understanding (generalizations and insights) to give meaning to the data. Most educational testing is aimed at assessing either information or understanding; to our way of thinking, this is just the first phase of the process of functional learning.

Linkage 3: From Understanding to Relevance

A large proportion of informational input is never assessed in terms of its relevance to the information holder's specific situation (or to the operation of an organization). One of the most important challenges for the consultant is to help client learners to establish this perception of relevance. Relatively few consultants stop regularly to ask client learners to reflect on ways in which the ideas being presented can be applied to their own situations and needs.

Linkage 4: From Relevance to Intention to Act

Another challenge for the consultant is to help establish a bridge from the client learner's perception of relevance to the potential use of the knowledge in action. After being presented with the linkage model, one of our European colleagues said, "I grew up in the coffee houses of Vienna. My friends and I could solve any problem of the world in three hours of any afternoon. We had very sophisticated awareness and could make any data relevant to our situations." However, when we asked him whether the coffee-house group ever enacted these solutions, he said, "No, never! We had solved the problems in our heads. That was enough for us."

Many case analyses and group discussions stop at this point without any linkage to an intention to do something. At this point in a consulting endeavor, we often find it important to legitimize ambivalence about risk taking as a normal condition. We use a variety of techniques to encourage "internal dialogue" between the cautious, protective elements and the risk-taking, proactive elements.

However, a proactive stance sometimes emerges as an impulsive act; and such acts are usually unsuccessful because they lack the guidance of problem-solving deliberation and sensitivity to the needs of others. The challenge for the consultant as trainer is to provide a linkage to exploring alternatives before jumping into action.

Linkage 5: From Intention to Act to Problem Solving and Goal Setting

Once the intention to act has been established, it is important that the consultant help the client to see that several alternative actions should be considered. This is a key intervention in many consulting and training situations. It may lead to exploring existing innovative solutions, brainstorming alternatives and assessing consequences, and/or doing feasibility analysis.

At this point in many consulting endeavors, one alternative is chosen and implemented. Such an action certainly has a higher probability of success than the trigger act, but still may be sadly lacking in terms of the quality of its implementation. The supportive consultant still has a lot of help to give to ensure success.

Linkage 6: From Goal Setting to Action Planning

Goal setting is the launching pad for creative and realistic, step-by-step action planning. This planning process includes not only the projected action sequence, but also consideration of others who need to be involved and the form that such involvement should take. Evaluation is also considered in terms of evidence of progress and how to celebrate steps toward progress. Celebration is important in that it provides the motivation to keep investing time and energy in the effort.

Linkage 7: From Action Planning to Rehearsal of Management Presentation

In teaching client learners how to present their action plan to top management for approval, it is crucial to provide an opportunity to practice the presentation and to develop any necessary skills in a risk-free situation, with a chance for feedback and further practice. The techniques of role playing, simulation, and guided imagery are useful at this stage.

Linkage 8: From Rehearsal to the Actual Presentation

The point at which client learners are ready to present their action plan to top management is not clear-cut. The learners must feel that they are ready and that they have developed appropriate levels of necessary skills, and the consultant must be willing to help with and support the decision.

Linkage 9: From Presentation to Action and Building Support

A good consultant helps the client learners to identify the necessary sources of support for the contemplated action and helps to develop a strategy for involving these sources in the action. For example, the consultant may emphasize to top management how important it is to listen receptively to the client learners' presentation and to collaborate with the presenters. Helping to prepare potential support systems for receptivity to the initiatives of the risk takers is one of the consultant's most critical responsibilities.

A PROCEDURE FOR DESIGNING LEARNING SESSIONS

After helping to design hundreds of learning sessions for all types of groups with a great variety of purposes, we have come to the conclusion that there are three essential stages to the designing of successful sessions and four kinds of decisions involved in every episode of designing. In the following paragraphs we briefly define the three stages, providing an excerpt of the planning sheet that we use during each, and describe the four kinds of decisions.

Stage 1: Preparation

Before starting the actual process of designing, the consultant must answer the following questions:

- What are the needs, interest level, and expectations of the client learners? What individual differences exist among the learners with regard to needs, interest level, and expectations?
- What possible outcomes of the session would actualize the needs and expectations of the learners and the planners?
- What are possible activities, materials, human resources, and agenda items that might facilitate the achievement of high-priority outcomes?

A portion of the planning sheet that we use in Stage 1 is presented in Figure 5.

Participants (how many, subgroupings, individual differences and needs)	Desirable Outcomes (skills, information, values, concepts, action plans)	Ways to Facilitate Outcomes (activities, resources, facilities, work groups)
• Seven department heads, each with two respected employees from the department • Two women and five men • Three new and four long-time employees * • Great individual differences in autocratic to democratic styles * • Some accustomed to planning with staff and others not	• To generate pool of ideas about how to improve morale and efficiency during next six months * • To arrive at recommendation about priority actions and who should be responsible • To help improve communication between department heads and between departments	* • Brainstorm causes of morale difficulties • Subgroups cutting across departments • Duplicating machine to duplicate task-force recommendations immediately * • "Stop session" to look at inhibitions and supports for open communication
* Consultant places asterisk next to most important characteristics and differences among participants to keep in mind.	* Consultant places asterisk next to highest-priority outcomes.	* Consultant places asterisk next to items that seem to be the most appropriate, effective, and feasible features of design.

Figure 5. Excerpt from Planning Sheet for Stage 1 (Preparation)

Stage 2: Construction

The second stage involves constructing the actual design for the session (or the sequence of sessions if more than one is necessary). In Stage 2 the consultant must answer these questions:

- How will the session begin?
- What is the estimated time for each of the activities under consideration?
- What activities, methods, and subgroupings will be used?
- Who is responsible for facilitating each activity?
- What are the necessary arrangements of space, equipment, and materials?

Figure 6 presents an excerpt from the planning sheet that we use in Stage 2.

Time Estimate (activities, methods, grouping)	Who Is Responsible	Arrangements of Space, Equipment, Materials
Presession and Start-Up		
1. *20 minutes:* People interview each other in pairs across departments; start as soon as one such pair has arrived	Consultant meets at door and gets people started	Interview schedule; chairs arranged for interviews; start-up instruction sheet; felt-tipped markers
Flow of Session After Start-Up Activities		
2. *10 minutes:* General session; welcome participants; remind participants of purposes described in agenda; introduction of department heads, who then introduce their people	Consultant	Seating at tables in groups of five or six; extra copies of agenda prepared and sent in advance
3. *25 minutes:* "Future-image" activity in which teams envision one year ahead; observe all evidences of high morale and productivity	Consultant, department heads	Newsprint and felt-tipped markers on each group's table
4. *20 minutes:* Image-of-future sheets posted; participants read and check most important items for priorities, etc.	Consultant	Newsprint to be posted on walls, felt-tipped markers for checking items on newsprint, masking tape, etc.

Figure 6. Excerpt from Planning Sheet for Stage 2 (Construction)

Stage 3: Follow-Up

This stage consists of providing follow-up and support so that the actions planned and the commitments made at the end of the session are carried out. This aspect of designing sessions is perhaps the most neglected, and it is also the most critical in terms of not wasting the learners' time and energy. The following questions must be answered:

- What kind of closure should there be for the session? What final commitments and evaluations should be made?
- What kind of follow-up support is needed to ensure that actions and commitments are carried out? Who is responsible for providing this support? Who will do what? When? Where?

A portion of the planning sheet applicable to Stage 3 is presented in Figure 7.

Four Kinds of Design Decisions

The four kinds of decisions involved in every episode of designing are as follows:

1. Decisions about arranging and using the physical facilities and arranging for the equipment that will best facilitate communication, involvement, and interaction;

---

1. **Plans for Ending Session** (closing activity, evaluation, etc.):
   - Department triads meet to plan first steps of action and then report these plans to everyone, including plans for continuing meetings and involving others; and
   - Sheet to evaluate the meeting distributed, completed by participants, and collected.

2. **Follow-Up Actions** (who will do what and when, plans, commitments, etc.):
   - Meeting in two months to report progress of plans;
   - Appointment of consultant to each team to support work and help to celebrate successes; and
   - Follow-up sending of instruments and other materials requested by any nonparticipants.

Figure 7. Excerpt from Planning Sheet for Stage 3 (Follow-Up)

2. Decisions about the flow of the work to be accomplished and the responsibilities to be fulfilled;
3. Decisions about the more specific designs of the various parts, modules, or building blocks of the total session (including considerations of sequence, content, and so forth); and
4. Decisions about specific actions or behaviors needed to initiate and facilitate the productive flow of the total session and its various parts.

FREEDOM TO CHANGE PLANS

We have discovered that consultants who use devices such as the planning sheets illustrated in Figures 5, 6, and 7 exhibit much more flexibility in revising their plans on the basis of feedback than do those who depend on spontaneity to guide them in leading sessions. Planning of the kind that we have illustrated provides the stimulus to think in terms of the needs and interests of the client learners as well as the security and confidence that form the basis for freedom to revise and change. The consultant must be able not only to plan thoroughly but also to change the plan when necessary and to determine what kind of change might be desirable.

TRAPS TO AVOID IN DESIGNING

There are a number of traps to avoid when designing and planning sessions:

1. Not obtaining data before the session about who the client learners are or why they are coming;
2. Not involving client learners in the planning of the session;
3. Omitting the designing procedure beforehand in the belief that, because a session occurs every week or every month, it is acceptable to make plans after people arrive;
4. Holding a session only because it is scheduled;
5. Failing to devise a definite way to begin the session (particularly when it is known that people may arrive at different times);
6. Not sharing the agenda with the learners·

7. Relying totally on one expert in attendance rather than using that person to help uncork the resources of all the learners;

8. Not dealing with the learners' feelings about the session content or the tasks to be accomplished;

9. Failing to ensure that visual aids are legible by testing them in the room in which the session is to be held;

10. Allowing long coffee breaks that are not part of the design of the session and that break up work processes and waste a great deal of time;

11. Arranging seating in such a way that people cannot see one another or cannot participate easily;

12. Not checking equipment before the session to ensure that it is working properly;

13. Not allowing the expression of individual preferences regarding what the learners might want to work on or which subgroups they would like to join;

14. Having no plans for transitions from one activity to another, one topic to another, or one session to another;

15. Skipping plans for follow-up, including determining and recording who will do what and when;

16. Using haphazard grouping patterns rather than giving thought to the best size and composition of subgroups for each task to be done;

17. Preparing inadequately for recording and distributing copies of the minutes or procedures of the session; and

18. Allowing the participation of an inadequately prepared, unknown, and uncomfortable resource person.

CHECK LIST FOR SESSION PLANNING

In planning sessions the consultant needs to consider such issues as the size of the client-learner group, the frequency with which the group may need to meet, the purpose and length of the session(s), and a number of other matters. Figure 8 presents a check list that the consultant may find helpful to use when planning sessions.

1. Notification

_____Notice(s)

_____Memorandum

_____Letter

_____Phone call

_____Personal contact

_____Bulletin board

_____Other:

2. Agenda and Other Resource Materials

_____Number of copies of agenda

_____Speeches

_____Minutes

_____Reprints

_____Reports

_____Other:

3. Responsibilities at the Meeting

_____Leader

_____Recorder

_____Resource person(s)

_____Observer(s)

_____"Hosting" rules

_____Other:

4. Examination of Physical Setting

_____Size of space

_____Electric outlets

_____Microphone facilities

_____Lighting

_____Acoustics

_____Climate controls

Figure 8. Check List for Session Planning

_____Doors

_____Bathrooms

_____Number of people who can be accommodated

_____Stairs

_____Elevators

_____Parking

_____Telephone access

_____Custodian/engineer

_____Separate rooms for subgroup work

_____Other:

5. Equipment

_____Tables

_____Chairs

_____Microphones

_____Audiotape recorder

_____Videotape recorder

_____Cassettes

_____Extension cords

_____Lectern

_____Easels

_____Film projector

_____Slide projector

_____Screen

_____Coffee/tea dispenser

_____Water pitchers

_____Chalkboard

_____Typewriters

_____Wastebaskets

_____Other:

Figure 8 (continued). Check List for Session Planning

6. Materials

_____Name tags/tents

_____Newsprint and flip charts

_____Felt-tipped markers

_____Masking tape

_____Blank paper

_____Pencils or pens

_____Visual aids

_____Books

_____Exhibit materials

_____Chalk

_____Other:

7. Final Check Before Session Starts

_____Seating arrangements

_____Extra tables and chairs

_____Public-address system

_____Equipment

_____Materials

_____Ashtrays

_____Water glasses

_____Climate

_____Coffee, tea, etc.

_____Other:

8. During the Session

_____Greeting and seating the learners

_____Establishing recording procedures

_____Greeting and including latecomers

_____Distributing materials

_____Other:

Figure 8 (continued). Check List for Session Planning

9. **After the Session**

_____Collecting used and unused materials

_____Returning equipment

_____Cleaning up

_____Establishing follow-up agreements

_____Other:

Figure 8 (continued). Check List for Session Planning

CONSULTANT ROLES
IN FACILITATING SESSIONS

Consultants may fulfill a number of different roles as they strive to involve client learners in sessions that result in high productivity:

1. ***Collector of Diagnostic Data.*** The consultant may collect feedback data from staff members about their evaluations of sessions and their ideas about changes that might make future sessions more worthwhile. Sometimes these data are collected through the medium of group interviews, other times through personal interviews, and sometimes through the administration of questionnaires. It is important that the consultant use the collected data to derive implications for specific improvement of session designs.

2. ***Designer and Leader.*** Sometimes the consultant bears the entire responsibility for designing and leading a session. Such a session may be a meeting of a committee or a task force or an ongoing staff unit.

3. ***Co-Planner.*** On some occasions the consultant helps to plan a session with the person who will serve as the session leader. In this role he or she functions as a design consultant, reacts to a tentative plan that the leader has developed, and/or helps with the session rehearsal to ensure that the design will be successful.

4. ***Process Observer.*** The consultant may be asked to observe a session and later provide feedback needed to improve the design of future sessions.

5. *Trainer of Facilitators.* Sometimes the consultant is in the fortunate position of designing and leading a training session for staff people on the techniques of designing and conducting good meetings.

REFLECTIONS ON THIS CHAPTER

It may seem at first thought that the designing of sessions is not critical to organization development. However, it is our experience that quite the opposite is true. Helping with the improvement of sessions often allows a nonthreatening entry into a system and affords visible and rapid success. In addition, this form of helping provides an excellent context in which to provide basic skill training for staff members without creating the kind of resistance that is often generated by other approaches to changing personal behaviors and values. In summary, this consultant function is often a successful first step that leads in many possible directions within the organizational system. Therefore, we strongly recommend that every consultant develop a strong repertoire of skills in designing sessions and in helping clients to provide competent and creative leadership in sessions.

Gordon: I'd like to emphasize again that entry into the system by helping to improve sessions may be one of the strategic organization-development interventions. Clients experience very visible and meaningful results by participating in this fairly safe improvement effort, which is relevant to all departments and units.

Ron: I have found that this intervention can be conducted in two ways. One way is to work with the group leaders of sessions, helping them go through a good design process. The other way is to work actively with the whole group, getting the members to participate in brainstorming about good and poor sessions, providing active facilitation of a good session, and then debriefing what made the session good and how to ensure that the positive elements can be carried forward in the future.

Gordon: I like the idea of working with the whole group on having a good session. You can help all the group members, including the leader, look at their own process and devise ideas for improving future sessions.

Ron: One thing that is often neglected is the importance of moving furniture around creatively to set up a good work space for communicating. Another important consideration is to have an easel, newsprint, and a felt-tipped marker ready for recording various kinds of information during the session.

Gordon: Another pitfall is forgetting to design the subgroup work needed to make the most productive use of people's time. I think that in most good sessions I've been involved with at least half of the time is spent in subgroup work—groups of three or four or small groups of people with similar interests. Subgroup work is just as important in problem solving as it is in learning groups.

REFERENCE

Cousins, N. (1981). *Human options.* New York: W.W. Norton & Company, Inc.

7

Diagnostic Analysis, Progress Assessment, and Evaluation

We believe that one of the most important roles of a good consultant is that of action-research leader in the data-collection activities of his or her work with a client. Kurt Lewin's concept of action research (Corsini, 1984) had as one of its core notions that when the client collaborates in collecting data, those data will have greater credibility, the client will be more willing to work on understanding them, and the client will be a more active participant in deriving the implications for action or change. Our experience indicates that a client can participate usefully in data collection by helping to:

- Determine the kinds of data needed in order to understand the problems being addressed;
- Figure out ways to acquire those data;
- Retrieve them;
- Analyze and summarize them; and
- Derive their most significant implications for a change effort.

This means that one of the functions of the consultant is to train research helpers in the skills and techniques needed for these data-collection activities. In many projects, for example, we have formed teams of client helpers and have trained these teams in interviewing skills; subsequently, the team members have conducted substantial interviews with samples of the client populations. We have had the content of these interviews checked against the work of professional interviewers and have always found comparable quality when our volunteer helpers had been through at least two training sessions with one trial interview in between.

KINDS AND SOURCES OF DATA

One pitfall for the consultant is developing too narrow a perspective with regard to the kinds and sources of data that might be relevant to the problem-solving effort. There is a tendency for consultants to think in terms of one or two conventional research techniques, such as administering questionnaires and conducting sample interviews, and to focus on a particular sample of the client population as the exclusive source of valid data. We have found that several different sources of data are needed in diagnosing a problem situation and helping to design plans for action:

1. *Traditions, Values, and Norms.* The traditions, values, and practices that represent the history and the ongoing maintenance of the organization are an excellent source of data. These elements of organizational life represent an equilibrium that, in Lewinian terms, maintains itself through a variety of forces that lead toward change and other forces that work against change.

2. *Goals, Objectives, and Policies.* The current goals, objectives, and policies that are supposed to be guiding the present activities of the organization are another valuable data source. These may, of course, exist at several levels of the system, such as the total organization, its subunits (divisions, departments, and so forth), its work groups, and its individual workers. In each of these levels are conflicts and ambivalence that need to be identified and explored.

3. *Problems and Concerns.* Data about the problems, concerns, frustrations, and feelings of pain with which the client is currently coping are significant. These phenomena may be quite different in different parts of the system (for example, among top managers as opposed to nonmanagerial employees or in the marketing function as opposed to the production function).

4. *Expectations of Customers and Potential Customers.* The desires and needs of these groups represent important aspects of the organization's environment.

5. *Assumptions About the Future.* The assumptions that are prevalent in the organization can provide additional data. These include beliefs about the future of the environment and the organization that may represent extrapolations of current social, economic, political, and technological trends.

6. *Scenarios of Desired Futures.* The organization's leaders and planners have undoubtedly developed such scenarios.

Other kinds and sources of relevant data certainly exist. Those listed above are only samples that have proved important to us in collecting the kinds of diagnostic data that have helped us to understand client systems and to develop collaborative plans for improvement efforts.

THE TARGETS OF DATA COLLECTION

The consultant must decide which parts and levels of the client system should be explored in order to assess the nature of the problems being coped with and the client's readiness to begin a change effort. There are a number of ways to approach this task. Some consultants, especially those with a clinical background, tend to focus much of their data collection on the individual "life spaces" of the workers—their motivations, their mental health, the quality of the work life they are experiencing, the types of rewards they receive, and their attitudes toward the organization's various employee-involvement activities. Other consultants feel that it is particularly important to focus on the groups and units of structure that make up the system, to explore the norms and expectations that have been developed and that support or inhibit group productivity. With the latter focus, data-collection efforts tend to concentrate on the group leadership and interpersonal relations that underlie teamwork.

Still other consultants feel most comfortable starting with some analysis of the dimensions of the total organization—the patterns of accountability in the top-management team, the way in which communication flows up and down, and the way in which decision making is structured and reinforced. Yet others prefer to focus on the larger systems that surround and influence organizational productivity and survival—communities, interorganizational relations, international corporations, and societal environments.

TOOLS, METHODS, AND DATA

"Hard-Data" Focus

Some consultants tend to focus their diagnostic efforts on "hard data." Their objective is to gather quantitative, reliable data from an adequate sample. They use methods that are standard and replicable in many situations and that are intended to answer the descriptive question "What is the situation now?" Such methods include precoded observations, carefully structured sample interviews, and analysis of documents using check lists for coding and analyzing data.

"Soft-Data" Focus

Other consultants tend to seek in-depth data about the complex of variables or dimensions of a situation by gathering information of a more personal nature. They collect anecdotal data from small samples, obtaining written descriptions of a situation so that they can analyze a client's readiness for change, what is hoped for, and what changes are desired.

These consultants interview groups of five or six people each, for example, and make observations of the types of interactions that occur in these groups as well as the actual information conveyed by the group members. They also hold informal, one-on-one conversations with employees in the client system and make notes about their observations. Instead of focusing on adequacy of the sample and reliability of the data, as is characteristic of consultants who seek "hard data," they are concerned with the richness and depth of the information they are collecting.

Intuitive-Synthesis Focus

More and more consultants are realizing the importance of trusting their intuition as a source of data. In fact, most effective consultations probably do not depend solely on a "left-brain" style of problem solving. The dictionary defines intuition as "quick perception of the truth without conscious attention or reasoning," "knowledge from within," and "instinctive knowledge or feeling associated with clear and concentrated vision." To many, intuition is a very meaningful process that produces unique and useful results. To others, because it is difficult to explain or prove, it is a suspect process that may lack validity.

The specific uses of intuition depend on the nature of each client and his or her concerns. A consultant is rarely in a situation in which the answers are clear. The process of seeking answers with the client by using intuition as well as other appropriate methods of inquiry encourages the client to trust his or her own intuition and thereby become more confident and self-sufficient. The client's capacity for creative self-renewal also is increased by being comfortable with the intuitive process.

Both rational and nonrational avenues can help a client to identify issues and develop alternative strategies for change; the dynamic interplay of intuition and analysis leads to the most effective outcome. It is our belief that a good consultant includes in his or her repertoire the tools and approaches of "hard-data" analysis, "soft-data" inquiry procedures, and the willingness to be open to intuitive synthesis.

THE GOALS AND LEVELS OF DATA COLLECTION

We believe that determining which data-collection procedures to use depends on which of the following goals the consultant wishes to accomplish:

- Diagnostic problem analysis;
- Progress assessment and documentation; or
- Outcome evaluation ("bottom-line" assessment).

We feel that it is much too vague to talk about evaluation methods and diagnostic procedures. In the paragraphs that follow, we discuss each of these goals separately, concentrating on how data may be collected according to the level of the organization that serves as the focus of the investigation: the individual, the group, the organization, or the macrosystem.

Diagnostic Problem Analysis

With this goal the consultant is usually interested in exploring some of the causes of the problem situation, such as blocks to productivity, barriers to good interpersonal and group relations, clarity of goals, the presence or lack of current images of future outcomes, the adequacy of leadership performance, and communication flow.

When the diagnostic focus is on the *individual,* the data-collection procedure may include intensive individual interviews, a questionnaire designed to reveal morale, or a check list of attitudes and concerns. The consultant may have a diagnostic interest in individual differences and may use such tools as the Myers-Briggs Type Indicator[19] to identify the clusters of individuals that make up the work force being studied. There may be a special interest in the quality of work life, attitudes and feelings, or conflicts between the work-related and the nonwork-related aspects of an individual's life. The consultant who is focused on individual diagnosis as an entry into providing help to an organization probably has a significant interest in the individual differences that need to be understood by management.

When the diagnostic focus is on *group* functioning and the various aspects of applied group dynamics, the consultant is likely to observe the group; conduct group interviews; and use various kinds of questionnaires to assess norms, supervision, goals, any blocks to communication that may be reducing productivity, and the informal power system.

When the diagnostic focus is on the functioning of the *organization* as a system, the consultant may use still other methods. The consultant who has a "hard-data" focus may interview or administer some type of questionnaire to a sample of the population. The consultant with a "soft-data" focus may select individuals from different parts of the structure to interview in depth about the functioning of some particular aspect of the system and the kinds of interactions that take place between or among parts of the system. In addition, the consultant may show a strong interest in establishing a picture of the way in which leadership functions at the different levels of the system and the kind of influence dynamics involved in both downward and upward communications. He or she may want to analyze the organization's mission statement and the way in which it seems to connect or not connect to the actual operations and the existing productivity level. The different products of organizational functioning, such as the annual report, newletters, and memoranda from top management, may be investigated as well.

When the focus is on *macrosystem* dynamics, diagnostic emphasis may be placed on the relationships of the organization to its environment, to other organizations, and to the economic and political functioning of the current society. The consultant also may examine the ways in which environmental scanning is conducted and the ways in which the resulting data are used in system planning. In addition, the consultant may analyze the kinds of societal, regional, and community trends that have

---

[19]The Myers-Briggs Type Indicator may be obtained from Consulting Psychologists Press, 577 College Avenue, Palo Alto, California 94306, phone (415) 857-1444.

an impact on the organization's functioning and its future. The search for data also may include analyses of relevant media, documentation about interorganizational relations and the organization's relationship to its market, political and economic leadership, and technological innovations.

Progress Assessment and Documentation

One of the responsibilities of the consultant is to help the client identify interim steps toward goal achievement and ways to assess or measure whether appropriate progress is being made. Included in this responsibility is the identification of ways to determine when the client is moving toward a dead end or toward unexpected consequences or obstacles.

In addition, the consultant needs to emphasize to the client how important it is to celebrate positive progress. In our work culture relatively little attention or priority is given to the notion of celebrating progress, even though such celebrations are crucial to continued motivation and renewal of efforts. One key part of this process is to ensure that evidence of each positive step taken is well documented and shared (with top management, for example) as part of a recognition-and-reward system.

When the focus of the progress assessment is on the *individual,* the consultant may use such procedures as repeat measurements of performance level, supervisors' reports of improvement in relation to goals set during performance-review sessions, and the individual's own reports on feelings of progress and changes in attitudes toward work life. Celebrations of individual progress may range from pats on the back by the supervisor to identification on bulletin boards or in newsletters, notes from management, and various other kinds of rewards.

Progress assessment at the *group* level may focus on collection of data concerning productivity or quality control (for example, facts about waste and rejects, progress on reducing absenteeism, and group members' ratings on satisfaction with their group and its productivity). One excellent way to approach assessment at this level is to have a group facilitator help the group examine its own process and make decisions about ways to improve its functioning. Every consultant needs to know how to set up such examination sessions and how to provide the tools for supporting them.

When the focus of progress assessment is on the *organization,* data can be collected about savings on overhead expenditures, quality production, production level, profit level, and success in trying out innovations in production and operating procedures. It is sometimes a good idea to use a panel of observers to review periodically what progress is being made within the organization. Also, data can be collected from both managerial and nonmanagerial employees concerning their assessment of progress made after a previous assessment point.

In attempting to collect information about progress at the *macrosystem* level, the consultant may use anthropological procedures to obtain information on the image of the organization held by insiders as well as that held by consumers of the organization's products. Another interesting kind of assessment consists of analyzing the degree to which the organization is taking the initiative to adapt innovations developed in other systems and, in addition, analyzing progress in competitive efforts or in collaborative efforts with other systems for mutual benefit.

Outcome Evaluation
("Bottom-Line Assessment")

A third purpose of data collection is to measure at some predetermined time the degree to which goals have been achieved and the degree to which "bottom-line" criteria have been met. Often the data needed for this purpose appear in an annual report or can be gleaned from a review of the success of strategic-planning efforts. Documentation is needed in order to be able to report what has been accomplished and how it was accomplished.

When an *individual* evaluation is needed, the consultant may obtain information from the record of the individual's annual review with his or her supervisor, which should contain data regarding the degree to which performance and personal-development goals have been achieved during the past year as well as data regarding areas for improvement. The "bottom-line" notion may apply to the degree to which the individual's resources are being adequately used or to the level of contributions that he or she is making to the objectives of the group and the organization involved.

At the *group* level, evaluation may focus on the productivity and commitment of one particular group or on a comparison of these elements within various groups that are carrying out similar tasks in the organization. Outcome evaluation at the level of the *organization* may be focused on the evidence of "bottom-line" results in terms of profit, level of waste, reduction in overhead, and the degree to which employees at all levels are concerned with the welfare of the organization. Evaluation of the functioning of the *macrosystem* may focus on the degree to which there is harmful, wasteful competition or beneficial collaboration between two or more neighboring systems or systems involved in the same type of "bottom-line" objectives.

RESEARCH ON EVALUATING THE CONSULTING PROCESS[20]

Despite the fact that virtually every kind of business, government, and service organization has been involved in consultation to some extent, only a limited amount of research exists on evaluating the consulting process. Our experience has indicated that evaluative research is needed by both the consultant and the client. Our first research study not only resulted in publication (Lippitt, 1959), but also was invaluable as action research on the client's problem.

The general literature on consulting has grown along with the professional practice. An extensive annotated bibliography on consultation was published in 1962 and revised in 1972 by the Bureau of Business and Economic Research, Graduate School of Business Administration, Michigan State University (Hollander, 1972). The number of entries increased from 478 in the 1962 edition to almost twice that number in the 1972 edition. However, about 85 percent of the entries were descriptive, theoretical, or case reports. Most of the research studies reported were done by private consulting firms and public agencies.

In a survey of consultants and clients (Bidwell & Lippitt, 1971) done at George Washington University, we found some key obstacles to research on the consulting process (see Table 1). According to the seventy-five people who were surveyed, the key obstacles were lack of time, inadequate frame of reference for evaluations, and inability to develop measurable objectives of the consultation. Although it is understandable that lack of time and money is important, it is interesting to note the number of respondents who indicated their inability to establish a frame of reference for conducting such research.

---

[20]Gordon Lippitt presented a portion of this section as a paper entitled "Research on the Consulting Process" at the annual conference of the Academy of Management, Orlando, Florida, August 1977.

Obstacles	Number of Responses (N = 52)*
1. Lack of time	20
2. Lack of frame of reference	15
3. Failure of consultant and client to determine client expectations in measurable terms	14
4. Lack of money for research	12
5. Need to convince management	9
6. Lack of effective research methods and tools	6
7. Need for adequate facilities and resources	3
8. Lack of cooperation between client and consultant	2
9. Magnitude of research	2

*Twenty-three respondents did not answer all the questions, and sixteen gave two or more responses.

Table 1. Obstacles to Consulting Research

A MODEL FOR EVALUATING THE CONSULTING PROCESS

A useful conceptual model (Swartz & Lippitt, 1975) for evaluating consultative efforts is shown in Figure 9. The following paragraphs offer definitions and brief explanations of the four interdependent elements that are diagramed in this figure.

Evaluation Areas

The following are the three major areas in which a consultative effort can be evaluated:

1. *Client/Consultant Relationship.* The relationships that exist among the client, the client system, and the consultant often have a major impact on the final outcome of the consulting process.

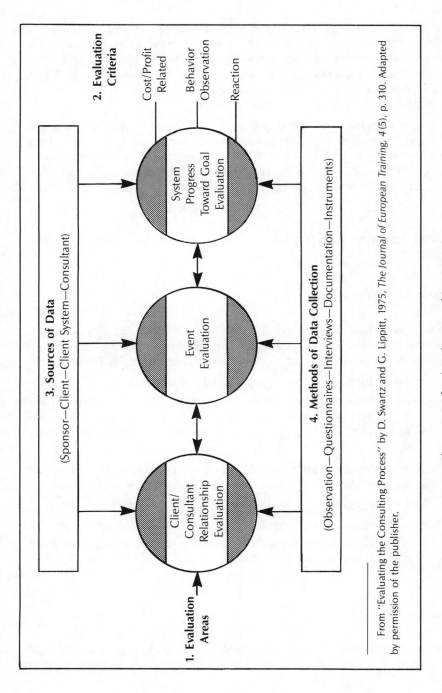

Figure 9. Evaluating the Consulting Process

From "Evaluating the Consulting Process" by D. Swartz and G. Lippitt, 1975, *The Journal of European Training, 4* (5). p. 310. Adapted by permission of the publisher.

2. *Consulting/Training Events.* This area covers significant consulting interventions, such as survey-feedback meetings, skill training, and conflict-resolution meetings. Assessing the impact of each of these events on the overall project can provide important information for use in designing future projects with the client and for improving similar events that will take place during the current project.

3. *Progress Toward Specific Goals.* This area relates to the degree to which the consulting effort has helped the client system to achieve progress toward its prestated goals. Evaluation of overall results helps to answer the client's question, "Was the money I invested in consultation returned, at least, by the results achieved?"

Evaluation Criteria

Cost/Profit

Some "hard-data" criteria may be developed to determine as directly as possible the effect of consultation on the achievement of specified results. Examples of specified results related to cost/profit are as follows:

- Consulting time and expense (estimated versus actual);
- Consulting-event outcomes that result in increased sales and/or decreased costs; and
- Changes in safety record, grievances, turnover, absenteeism, and theft.

When evaluating a consultative effort according to cost and/or profit concerns, the consultant may use one of three approaches to measurement:

- Specific goal attainment by a specified time;
- Tracking of trends versus a plan or estimated performance; and
- Spot checks of performance versus hoped-for change (for example, the reversal of a downward trend).

Behavior

A consultative effort may be evaluated according to significant changes in individual, group, or organizational behavior that resulted directly from the consulting process or from an event influenced by the consulting process. Some examples of observed behavioral changes are as follows:

- The client is much more relaxed and is functioning in a more assertive manner;
- A change has occurred in the organization's structure, simplifying lines of communication; and
- Client learners demonstrate that they can plan for and conduct problem-solving meetings.

Reactions

The reactions of the client and the client system to the consulting process may be evaluated. Members of the client system may report feelings, attitudes, and points of view as these change over time. The kinds of reactions that may be evaluated are as follows:

- The client's expressed feelings about the consulting relationship;
- The client learners' evaluation of a training event; and
- The reactions of members of the client system as expressed through a series of attitude surveys during the course of the consulting process.

Sources of Data

There are four sources of data for an evaluation of a consulting effort:

1. ***The Sponsor.*** The sponsor can significantly influence the consulting process and has a strong interest in its initiation, progress, and final outcome. In some instances the sponsor is the client's supervisor; many times, particularly when the consultant is working with top management, the sponsor is the client (for example, the president of the organization). The sponsor also may be a group, such as a city council, an advisory board, an executive committee, or a board of directors.

2. ***The Client.*** This person approves or denies approval of various events and directions within the sphere of the consulting project.

3. ***The Client System.*** This person or group is directly involved in, or affected by, the consulting project.

4. *The Consultant.* This is the person for whose time and expertise the client has contracted. The consultant may be internal or external to the client system; there may be a combination of internal and external helpers.

Methods of Data Collection

Data can be collected in a wide variety of ways. The following are five methods that are most frequently used to collect data for evaluating the consulting process:

1. *Observation.* Individual and group behavior is observed and recorded as it relates to the job to be done. Also observed and recorded are the ways in which systems are functioning, as indicated by flow charts, decision trees, and PERT[21] charts.

2. *Questionnaires.* Formats are specially designed or standardized, asking for individual written responses concerning attitudes, viewpoints, opinions, and perceptions.

3. *Interviews.* Individuals or groups are interviewed face to face or by telephone to obtain their in-depth perceptions, specific examples, ideas, and feelings.

4. *Documentation.* Archival records, current records, and specially recorded data are used to show trends and changes resulting from the consulting process.

5. *Instruments.* Devices are specially designed to obtain individual feedback about a situation and to provide a framework for evaluation discussions among the client, the client system, and the consultant.

It is interesting to note in Table 2 that, although a number of additional data-collection methods were listed in the Bidwell and Lippitt (1971) survey, questionnaires were the most frequently cited.

At this point it should be reiterated that every consulting situation is a data-collection process. In fact, the Bidwell and Lippitt survey showed that action research was the most frequently mentioned purpose for data collection in the consulting relationship (see Table 3). However, there is

---

[21]For a brief explanation of PERT, read "An Introduction to PERT. . .or. . ." by D.E. Yoes in *The 1972 Annual Handbook for Group Facilitators* (pp. 135-137) by J.W. Pfeiffer and J.E. Jones (Eds.), 1972, San Diego, California: University Associates.

Methods	Number of Responses (N = 64)*
1. Questionnaires	32
2. Interviews	16
3. Client reports	14
4. Efficiency reports	10
5. Discussions with client	9
6. Periodic testing	9
7. Inspections and visits	8
8. Consultant's ratings	8
9. Postevaluations immediately after consultations	7
10. Surveys of reactions to consultations	7
11. Surveys and operations audits	4
12. Follow-up testing (six months to one year later)	1

*Eleven respondents did not list any methods, and thirteen listed four different methods.

Table 2. Methods Used for the Evaluation of Consultation

Purposes	Number of Responses (N = 75)*
1. Action research on the problem	68
2. Evaluation of the consulting process	55
3. Satisfaction of client	53
4. Improved skill or performance of consultant	38
5. Other	23

*Fifty-four respondents indicated three or more purposes for evaluating consultation, and fourteen listed five purposes. The category "Other" included such purposes as increased business income, change in organizational relationships, value to organization, results in productivity and profits, program results, relationship to mission objectives, and supervisor's appraisal of value of consultation.

Table 3. Purposes for the Evaluation of Consultation

some difficulty in attempting to look at action research as simply a research method or a technology of consultation because the total consultation process is essentially a program of action research.

REFERENCES

Bidwell, R., & Lippitt, G. (1971). *Attitudes of consultants and clients to research on the consultation process.* Unpublished manuscript, George Washington University, Washington, DC.

Corsini, R.J. (Ed.). (1984). *Encyclopedia of psychology* (Vol. 1) (pp. 11-13). New York: John Wiley.

Hollander, S.C. (Compiler). (1972). *Management consultants and clients.* East Lansing, MI: Michigan State University Press.

Lippitt, G.L. (1959). A study of the consultation process. *Journal of Social Issues, 15*(2), 43-50.

Swartz, D., & Lippitt, G. (1975). Evaluating the consulting process. *Journal of European Training, 1*(3), 286-301.

8

Examples of Consultation in Action

In this chapter we share one full case study and a series of consultation vignettes involving different types of clients with varying needs. We also share comments about our intentions and intervention decisions with regard to these examples.

A CASE STUDY

The Organization Involved

This case study involves a lengthy and continuing consultation process with a large social-welfare organization. This organization has a national headquarters with 655 employees; in addition, there are four regional operations and an overseas division. The regional offices have over one thousand paid employees, and a field staff of several hundred people provides direct supervision and consultation to 3,700 local units of the organization. It is estimated that over two million volunteers are involved in the local, regional, and national-headquarters operations.

Stimulating a Need for Change in the Organization

The organization's management personnel requested that the training staff study existing organization development (OD) practices and theories in industrial, educational, and voluntary organizations. Subsequently, the training staff selected a committee whose members represented all levels of management from the vice president to local-unit executives. This committee's tasks were to become familiar with popular practices and theories, conduct a survey to examine existing management needs within the organization, and recommend a program whereby these needs could be met. The formulation of the committee developed a readiness on the part of management to examine the best ways to develop leaders in the organization, become involved in the assessment process, and use the committee's findings. With a client system of this scope, it seemed to us crucial to assemble an inside team to communicate with the units of the system during all phases of the project. Without this support, data collection and action planning would be difficult.

For many years the organization had been carrying out a program in orientation training, on-the-job training, and training in specialized vocational skills. A management survey that had been conducted previously in connection with this program provided additional force during the "readiness phase." Although very few of the recommendations resulting from the earlier survey had been implemented in the organization's normal, day-to-day operation, it was recognized that they might be meaningful. The credence afforded these earlier recommendations, as well as the predisposition to believe that the results of the new survey also might be meaningful, affected the organization's readiness for consultation; consequently, we were called in to help review the committee's recommendations and to explore ways of implementing them. The implication of this experience is that sometimes a consultant fails to explore significant, unused data that not only can provide an excellent diagnostic start-up but also can ease a client's feelings of guilt about not having benefited sufficiently from a previous effort.

Developing and Defining the Helping Relationship

The helping relationship with the organization changed as its needs grew and developed and the demands for its work in society changed. The relationship became defined in working with the organization.

The initial helping relationship involved the efforts of a consultant in planning a management-training activity. Working with the committee, the consultant helped assess the basic needs for such training. The following conclusions were reached:

- The managers needed increased awareness of the effects of managerial behaviors on subordinates; increased skill in diagnosing the work situation in which they operated; and increased understanding of the nature of a modern, complex organization and of the action necessary to achieve the organization's goals effectively.
- The managers' technical skills, such as budgeting and time planning, could be effectively used only if the managers also developed certain insights and understandings.
- The emerging body of information in the behavioral and management sciences about the nature of an organization and how people behave at work should be available as a primary resource in the design of any OD effort.

In light of these conclusions, the committee recommended an OD effort based on long-range planning rather than a "quick-fix" approach. On the basis of this recommendation, management decided to support a three-year program in the field of management development. The managers thought that such a period of time would allow effective evaluation of the program. They also believed that it would afford an opportunity to conduct a real test of the methods and philosophy being used in carrying out management training and OD processes.

In planning the management-training program, we recognized that it could benefit from the participation of outside specialists in fields such as public administration, social work, business administration, sociology, psychology, and so forth. In addition, as the program progressed, other consultants were made available to different levels of the organization in an effort to help them use the various specialists to the greatest advantage. This consultative function added another dimension to the helping relationship; we were able to refer the client to other resources.

Another phase of the helping relationship, which emerged after the initial three-year effort, resulted from the widening interest in organizational training and the recognized need for a continual relationship with consultants. The organization hired a group of three "core consultants" who worked together to develop a philosophy and methods of consulting for the organization. These three people had skills in the areas of research, education, training, community organization, and management. Although the core consultants were frequently assigned to work on special projects as individuals, they maintained a close working relationship with one another and kept in close contact with the organization's training function so that the total needs of the organization would be met. An outside team such as that formed by the three consultants is usually needed in a project of this scope; in addition, the teamwork exhibited by the members of the consulting team becomes a model for the client's own internal resource teams.

Clarifying the Nature of the Difficulties

The committee's work with the consultants clarified a number of difficulties within the organization:

1. ***Distance Between the Policy Makers and the Implementers.*** Questionnaries, interviews, and reports indicated that one of the existing problems was the distance between the policy makers at the national level and the ultimate consumers in the local units. This distance caused misunderstanding, resistance, and poor communication in the work of the organization at the community level.

2. ***Isolation and Competition Among Various Units.*** In a large organization that has many units responsible for several different programs, competition among the various units is almost inevitable. Here it was evidenced by a lack of intercommunication about programs plus the inability of many participants at the local-unit level to focus on the "total picture" of the organization and its work.

3. ***Communication Difficulties Between Different Hierarchical Levels.*** Four levels of hierarchy in the organization—the national headquarters, the regional offices, the field staff, and the local units— posed numerous communication problems. Although newsletters, management directives, and other media were used, face-to-face communication among members of the various levels was limited.

4. ***Remote Supervision.*** The problem of remote supervision was most evident in the relationship between the members of the field staff, who were constantly "on the road," and their supervisors in the regional offices. Although this arrangement permitted a great deal of freedom, it prevented good communication, in-service development, and an effective relationship between supervisors and their subordinates.

5. ***Ineffective Relationships Between Volunteers and Paid Staff.*** The volunteers, some of whom were the basic policy makers on the organization's national board, were also a real part of the "staff," from national headquarters down to the local-unit level. However, the problems of perception, recognition, authority, and role relationship between the paid and the volunteer staffs persisted, despite the organization's history of effective use of volunteers.

This problem is, of course, typical of nearly every agency that uses volunteers. However, in this case it was especially significant because the volunteers were integrated into all levels of the organization; consequently, relationship problems existed in many different personnel situations.

6. *Lack of Training Standards.* Extensive training went on throughout the organization, particularly in the program-service areas, with most of the program segments taking responsibility for training within their own areas of specialty. However, it was obvious to the committee that a need existed to develop common standards for these various kinds of training and to exercise some control over the development of trainers.

7. *Failure to Meet Widening Training Needs.* In the past the internal trainers had tended to be perceived as somewhat low in the organizational hierarchy. However, the widening interest in and need for training made imperative a broader base of qualified trainers at various organizational levels. In addition, any new programs to be implemented would require the existing training staff to achieve higher levels of proficiency.

8. *Lack of Effective Human Relations.* The committee's assessment indicated a clear need for improved interpersonal relationships at all work levels so that the organization could more effectively meet the obligations of its programs.

This summary of difficulties represents a good level of system thinking, demonstrates the need for acceptance of these difficulties as legitimate, and provides sufficient stimulus for determining implications for action in sessions with several different strategic groupings.

Setting Change Intentions

Although the original consultation process was initiated in connection with management-training possibilities, during its three-year period the need for other kinds of changes became apparent. Not only did the managers begin looking at their responsibilities in light of a better concept of themselves and their working relationships with others; but also they became aware of the potential for developing human resources and the role of trainers within the organization. This experience bears out our belief that a fully participative diagnostic phase is the best way to create the readiness for change, to develop the credibility of the helpers, and to foster the awareness of the need for technical help in the implementation phases of the change process.

Transforming Change Intentions into Change Efforts

As the ever-widening possibilities came into focus, several activities and changes developed:

1. *Perpetuation of the Management-Training Program.* After the three-year phase of the management-training program and the evaluation of its results, demands came from all parts of the organization to continue the program and to expand the training to the lower levels of supervision.

2. *Establishment of a Field-Staff Training Project.* The change in the organization's atmosphere as well as a study of local units showed a need to train the field-staff personnel, some of whom worked with eight to twenty of the local units. Because hiring sufficient numbers of consultants to do this training was a financial impossibility, the decision was made to institute a five-year, peer-training program. Each year thirty field-staff personnel were to be trained in certain curriculum areas of field-staff skills; then these thirty were to train others in their particular regions.

3. *Organization Development Projects.* As a result of the increasing importance of the training in organizational change, four of the organization's own program areas developed projects to meet their particular operational needs.

4. *Development of a National Training Council.* This council, which was developed to represent the entire organization, included members from local units, regional offices, program areas, and management as well as the four highest agency officials. It became a powerful force for initiating organizational change. With fifty representatives of both policy makers and implementers, the council was, in a very real sense, recommending action to itself. As a result of the continuing value seen in the council's training and OD efforts, training to meet various needs was revitalized at all levels.

Generalizing and Stabilizing Organizational Change

As implementation initiatives develop, the external consultant's role becomes one of consulting with internal leadership teams and helping to ensure the quality of action by attending to issues regarding process consultation and by helping to stabilize the changes that have been instituted. With this client this phase of the change process assumed different dimensions:

1. *Stabilizing the Effects of the Management-Training Program.* Interest in leadership training was heightened for most people, both lay and professional.

2. *Improving and Stabilizing the Functions of the National Training Council.* The national training council meets irregularly. In its first year it found itself somewhat hampered by the lack of work accomplished by subunits of the committee between meetings. As a result, a number of program-unit committees and interprogram task forces were set up to explore and carry out the national council's recommendations.

3. *Strengthening the Regional Training Committees.* In each of the regional offices, the regional training director and the regional manager had developed an area training committee. Interest was created through the national training council and in the training program. Throughout the organization there was a revitalization of interest in the regional training committees. This interest tended to stabilize the responsibility for training and to give greater support for the implementation of many activities.

4. *Upgrading the Role of Training Directors.* There was a recognition of the importance of training and the people who fulfill this function. This recognition resulted in higher status for the training directors and the training office.

5. *Expanding the Program for Training Trainers.* As basic program needs developed, trainers were trained accordingly.

6. *Developing a Philosophy of Training.* As a result of the many training activities, it was seen as necessary to create an organizational philosophy of training operations. Consequently, the national training council formulated the basic elements of this philosophy, which reflected some of the organizational change that had taken place and demonstrated the insight and understanding that had developed from the OD consulting process in the organization. Some of these elements were as follows:

- Training should be action oriented in order to meet people's individual needs as well as the basic program needs of the organization;

- Training should be provided under circumstances that resemble as closely as possible those of the situations for which that training is developed;
- Outside resources should be used effectively to aid in the creative development of people within the organization;
- People who will be affected by the training should be involved in the planning and development of the training program;
- Training should be the job of everyone—supervisor, volunteer leader, manager, and field staff;
- Training should be decentralized;
- A training program should remain flexible and adjustable to meet the changing needs of the organization in the society in which it finds itself; and
- Training is an active process that should be experientially based and related to specific organizational situations.

In the later stages of consultation, one of the priorities becomes the "prevention of entropy," that is, maintaining the momentum and the vitality of the change process and preventing good starts from deteriorating.

Changing the Helping Relationship

In the seven years that have elasped in the ongoing consulting relationship with this organization, three important changes have emerged:

1. *Changes in the Expertise of the Organization's Training Staff.* In the early phases of the consultation process, the training staff perceived the resource consultants as "experts." The training staff now has more of the technical know-how that was first brought to the organization by the consultants. This transfer of expertise has created less dependency on the technical assistance of the consultants.

2. *Changes in the Role of the Core Consultants.* In the early period of the consulting relationship, the core consultants tended to be "doers" in various training activities. Now, however, as the organization concentrates on developing its internal training staff and as training spreads throughout the organization, the talents of the core consultants are needed in planning, in long-range development, and in thinking through organizational problems rather than in implementing training activities.

3. *Development of an Organizational Resource Network.* After the organization recognized the importance of using resource con-

sultants when appropriate, it developed a network of resources (in the universities, colleges, and organizations across the country that were geographically close to the local units of the organization). These resources are now available to help any level of the organization at the appropriate time and under certain circumstances.

These changes illustrate three of the greatest contributions of an external consultant: (1) a well-trained internal team of consultants, (2) good communications to a variety of external resources, and (3) clear conceptions on the part of organizational members regarding when to ask for help and where to obtain it.

Reflections on the Case Study

Ron: I would guess, Gordon, that the modeling of "non-ego-invested" teamwork on the part of the external consulting team had more of an impact than comes through in this case study.

Gordon: I think that's probably true. Certainly a strong internal team developed, and this internal team was able to give very competent consultative help after we withdrew. The members of the internal team continued to feel free to ask us for reactions in a very open way.

Ron: One of the things I hope our readers will identify with is the responsibility to document and share their experiences.

Gordon: This kind of sharing is more than just a service to others; it's a major way of learning from what you are doing.

CONSULTATION VIGNETTES

In each of the following short examples, we have attempted to focus on one or more core aspects of the intervention and then have commented on our perceptions of key aspects of the consultation.

Vignette 1: Building on Strengths

Concerned executives have always been challenged by the problems of integrating talents, making conflict constructive, and channeling human efforts toward organizational goals. A sizable (and profitable) service organization recently initiated a coordinated program of management by objectives (MBO) and OD in an effort to address some of these concerns. The program implementation was broken down into five phases.

Phase 1: Identifying Common Denominators

During this process individuals from all departments in the organization identified organizational goals that they felt were important. The input of these individuals was used to form a group consensus of primary goals with which most of the people in the company could identify. This step provided a base and a common denominator through which people could interrelate.

Phase 2: Completing Inventories of Organizational Strengths and Human Resources

This phase helped to identify resources within the organization that could be directed toward the accomplishment of its goals. Inventories were used to help reveal previously untapped capabilities and interests of the work force. These inventories fostered greater awareness of the total potential of the work force and helped in the redistribution of responsibilities.

Phase 3: Establishing Objectives

Measurable departmental and individual objectives were established to help channel individual and group resources toward agreed-on objectives. This process also helped to reinforce commitment through participation.

Phase 4: Measuring Results

Results were measured on the basis of group as well as individual performance. The participants themselves developed and agreed on these standards of evaluation, thus instituting a "self-policing" concept into the program that also improved individual motivation.

Phase 5: Reinforcing Good Results

Performance planning and employee appraisals emphasized the strengthening of good performance rather than the disciplining of poor behavior. This tended to build rather than destroy people's self-images and increased their ability to contribute.

The long-term results of the program have yet to be measured. There are, however, some good indications that support the following theories:

- People *do* tend to support changes in which they participate.
- Most people *do* want to do a good job (given the opportunity and assistance that they need).
- People need encouragement more than they need criticism.
- Programs involving MBO and OD tend to support each other.
- Real participation is a strong motivator.
- Building on strengths *is* better than focusing on weaknesses.

Reflections on Vignette 1

Gordon: What most organizations neglect is the inventing of available and unused personnel resources.

Ron: Yes, I agree, and some organizations that try it depend on gleaning this information from individuals who are too modest about or unaware of their personal strengths and assets. I have found that pairing workers who know each other and having them interview each other is an excellent procedure for determining unused resources.

Gordon: Certainly agreement on standards of evaluation and how to implement measurement is crucial; otherwise, this process of building on strengths just won't work.

Ron: Paying attention to recognizing and celebrating good performance—individual and group—has a powerful impact and is usually neglected.

Vignette 2: Conducting a Renewal Effort in a Successful Enterprise

It may not seem that an organization that is growing, profitable, and in the top one hundred on the Fortune 500 list needs a renewal program.

However, a combination of OD interventions over a period of three years in such an organization resulted in top management's participation in a multiorganizational program called ITORP (Implementing the Organizational Renewal Process). The ITORP program was an educational experience that capped the three-year effort and paved the way for ongoing renewal and practices.

Initially, a group of department heads at the director level attended a briefing session on confronting conflict and coping with change. This session broke the ice and led to massive management and organization development efforts over the three-year span. At the various divisions, middle managers attended "train-the-trainer" sessions to ensure that training and development responsibilities were being met. The emphasis was on experiential learning and content/process approaches to group dynamics. Simultaneously, front-line supervisors at two plant locations participated in a five-part, developmental-learning experience with supervisors and other line managers serving as group-discussion moderators. Everyone in management, including the plant managers, became involved in these programs as either resource or participant.

Personnel managers at manufacturing locations became training and development resources. Although they did not conduct sessions, they served in an advisory capacity to ensure that physical as well as material needs were met. They also underwent training to become change agents or internal consultants in preparation for expanded service to line management. In addition, more than seventy line managers conducted development sessions based on local and common problems. This entire approach is credited with increasing motivation and profitability throughout the organization.

Reflections on Vignette 2

Ron: No matter how successful the enterprise is, it is usually possible to provide interaction with the leadership of other enterprises that are clearly more productive or innovative in some areas of operation. That's what happened when people in this organization participated in the ITORP program with managers of other companies.

Gordon: When people become involved in a good experiential program, the insights and sense of growth will provide rewards, challenges, and the desire to learn more.

Ron: One thing to remember is that everyone won't be ready to become involved at the outset. Start-up should be for those who are ready, and these people should be given a chance to communicate and demonstrate the payoffs they are experiencing.

Vignette 3: Sharing Problems and Solutions

Twenty-seven directors and representatives of eleven departments and agencies from a large, suburban county participated in a two-and-one-half-day workshop on organizational renewal. Represented were personnel, the police, the water and sewage department, planning, the county executive office, the fire department, welfare, and the school system. This program, designed by Gordon Lippitt and Leslie This, has been successfully conducted with over three thousand managers and supervisory personnel in industrial, educational, governmental, and health-care systems.

The upper-echelon participants in this workshop reviewed their organizations' management processes and practices (communication, decision making, teamwork, and so forth), diagnosed problem areas, and planned corrective action. The county executives explored the issues of taxpayer revolt, lack of growth in housing, consumer expectations, the need for interdepartmental collaboration, resistance to centralization of budget and records, the need for performance accountability, as well as other problems affecting public-service agencies in the current economic and social climate.

Many of the workshop participants expressed high interest in the opportunity to share common problems with other county departments and to explore workable solutions to these problems. The dynamics set up by this historically unprecedented interaction made the workshop program refreshing and enjoyable as well as serious in intent and comprehensive in scope. A number of the departments are planning to conduct the workshop for their nonmanagerial employees.

The final session of the workshop provided the participants with an opportunity to plan actual change projects and to obtain consultation on their analyses and diagnoses of the forces with which they would have to contend in order to achieve the desired changes.

Reflections on Vignette 3

Ron: Employees within many organizations are eager to share and learn from one another if the procedure for doing so can be legitimized and made concrete enough that ideas can actually be adopted. Typically personnel do not initiate requests for such sharing. In this workshop, though, the conditions for asking for this kind of help were modeled and facilitated.

Gordon: Yes, the staff had to model probing questions to discover the specifics that lay behind the generalizations. Several times reports of workable solutions led to brainstorming alternative ideas.

Ron: Actually helping the participants plan back-home applications is a great support for using what is learned.

Gordon: Yes, when you conduct a workshop like this, you have to recognize and legitimize ambivalence about risk taking and have peers consult with one another about strategies.

Vignette 4: Implementing Change in a Higher-Education Setting

As a year-long project in organizational renewal neared completion at a community college in North Carolina, recommendations from seven task forces within the institution were readied for submission and evaluation.

The project began with two workshops, whose participants included a number of faculty members, administration staff, and students. In turn, the workshops led to establishing the task forces to begin a year of systematic study on a wide range of college procedures, activities, and problems.

The major goals of the workshops were to identify institutional problems that needed attention; to practice, under supervision, the processes for working on problems; to learn skills for problem solving; and to come up with recommendations for action.

The workshops provided the subjects for task forces. Lists of these subjects were circulated around the college, and people were encouraged to participate in task forces that reflected their special interests or concerns. The hope was and is to have many people involved in the project; the various task forces comprised up to ten members each, including a clerk and a consultant. These members included faculty, administration, staff, personnel, students, members of the board of trustees, and secretaries. The areas of study included instruction, planning, faculty orientation, structuring of authority and decision making, improved maintenance and beautification of campus grounds, increased use of on-campus space, equipment and facilities, and two-way communication.

The director of the advanced studies program at this college served as process consultant to the task forces. This individual believed that although the institution was strong, it needed to practice constantly those problem-solving skills that allow the fullest use of human resources.

Reflections on Vignette 4

Gordon: The toughest challenge in implementing change in a situation like this is to get the client participants beyond the talking stages.

Ron: One positive aspect in this case is that they voluntarily chose the areas of change they wanted to work on.

Gordon: But I don't have the feeling that they were working strategically on how to influence upward so that their recommendations would be listened to and acted on.

Ron: They did have a process consultant who saw it as his job to help develop skills of exerting influence. That's a step beyond what is done in most such projects.

Gordon: I wonder if he can help the trustees and administrators to see their challenge as listening and probing nondefensively when recommendations are presented and rewarding the task forces for their hard work.

Vignette 5: Devising an Executive-Development Model

Recognizing the need for giving attention to the "whole person" in training and developing managers, one international corporation has taken the following action:

- Created an executive-development model that gives equal emphasis to technical skills, organizational understanding, and human effectiveness (see Figure 10);

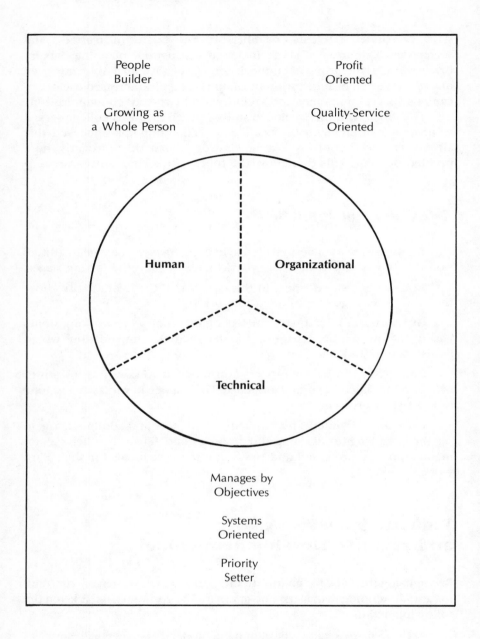

Figure 10. Executive-Development Model

- Developed an executive profile on each key manager identifying his or her strengths and weaknesses in each of these three areas;
- Made an inventory of each key manager's career goals, interests, geographic preferences, and so forth; and
- Established a professional-development plan for each key manager that outlines planned experiences, seminars, workshops, self-study, and so forth.

The purposes of this plan are as follows:

- To integrate personal and organizational goals whenever it is practical to do so;
- To help people develop the skills needed in positions before they are moved into these positions (to avoid promoting on the basis of irrelevant experience); and
- To develop more well-rounded managers at a variety of levels.

This company believes that a person's technical expertise will be more effectively applied if he or she understands how this expertise relates to the entire organization. Furthermore, the organization believes that it will be effective only to the degree that the members of its management team can interact maturely.

Reflections on Vignette 5

Ron: This is a description of a very interesting and significant outcome of a consultation process. How did the organization become interested in developing its managers in this way?

Gordon: The CEO and the vice president of human resources had attended a conference at which a paper was given on the three aspects of executive development. They asked me to help develop the model.

Ron: What would you say were your key interventions?

Gordon: First, I helped to set up some sessions attended by five to seven executives each. These executives were presented with the idea of creating an executive-development model and then brainstormed the contents of the model as shown in the figure. These contents were then edited by a team of three, and a copy of the resulting model was given to each executive to prepare a list of personal strengths and needs for growth. Each executive shared this list in a conference with a peer and his or her supervisor in order to refine it. Then the threesome listed professional-development priorities and possible growth experiences that could match these priorities. Each executive then chose two peers to help him or her monitor and debrief these growth experiences.

Ron: That sounds like a good application of participative-management thinking.

Vignette 6: Developing an Organization Through Personnel Development

Traditionally, hospitals have encouraged the professional and vocational growth of their employees as a means of improving the quality of patient care and the efficiency of the institution. This has been done in the belief that an employee's competence will increase and performance will improve in direct proportion to increased knowledge and improved skills. This theory is usually implemented in the traditional ways—by organizing in-service programs; conducting seminars; supplying employees with periodicals and films; sending them to national and regional meetings and conferences; paying their tuition fees for job-related technical and college courses, and so forth.

Until recently one large suburban hospital accepted this theory without question. However, as part of an ongoing quality-evaluation program undertaken by its board of trustees, the hospital began to critically examine this theory. Employee motivation, communication, supervisory skills, interpersonal and interdepartmental relationships as well as employee attitudes about their jobs, their fellow workers, their supervisors, and the institution itself were examined. It was discovered that increasing professional competence does not necessarily have an impact on complex intrahospital relationships, which directly affect the quality of care rendered and the efficiency of the organization.

The hospital remained committed to the more traditional goals and methods of professional and vocational growth, but it sought a means of evaluating more complex organizational needs. After several false starts, it became apparent that the hospital lacked the expertise to properly evaluate these complex needs. Consequently, a private consulting firm was hired to assist the evaluation process.

Moving the organization from a formalistic, direct-line management posture toward a participative one was one of the major evaluation goals.

Now supervisors are more confident of their managerial skills, more willing to delegate responsibility and authority, and more open to discussion of controversial issues. This transition was achieved through training sessions for every level of personnel, from the eight-member executive council to rank-and-file employees. As the program progressed through its various stages, supervisors and other employees were given special training by outside consultants and, in turn, have become training leaders themselves.

The hospital's ultimate goal is the development of a cadre of internal trainers to ensure program continuation without the assistance of outside consultants. With the help of the outside team, some criteria were developed for identifying staff members with the potential to become trainers. Independent ratings of staff members' potential were made by at least two insiders and two outsiders, and there was significant agreement on those with high potential. The names of those selected were first presented to their supervisors to obtain approval for approaching them. Then each potential trainer was interviewed about his or her interest in spending ten to twenty days per year as a member of the trainer network. Almost all were pleased with the opportunity and challenges of this additional role. They readily agreed to participate in a program to learn how to become trainers and an initial co-training session with an experienced trainer.

Reflections on Vignette 6

Ron: Adding line personnel to the trainer team as part-time contributors is one of the most significant innovations I have been involved in during the last few years. Not only does the quality of training in the system improve, but the management ratings of those who become involved in training go up very significantly.

Gordon: Yes, I've noticed that more of them are promoted to other line positions, and some start new careers as internal OD staff members.

Ron: It seems clear that line managers who have teaching and consulting skills are more productive as managers in participative-management systems.

9

Guidelines
for International Consulting[22]

An increasing number of consultants working in cross-cultural settings are finding that there are unique dynamics in such consultations. We already know something about the multiple difficulties that can be encountered in helping a human system—be it individual, group, organization, or community—in one's own culture without creating suspicion, hostility, or dependence. International consulting is infinitely more difficult. The international consultant faces different types of political systems, cultural variances, language barriers, national prides, contrasting ways of doing business, and other harsh realities (Harris, 1982).

As an international consultant who has fallen into the traps inherent in these realities, I would like to present a few of the more critical issues I have faced and some suggestions regarding ways to cope with them. Although these guidelines are couched in prescriptive language, I must acknowledge that there is no one right way to handle the problems that inevitably arise in cross-cultural helping. Circumstances vary tremendously, and in some situations the opposite of what I suggest may be the better approach. Nevertheless, I feel that any cross-cultural consultation depends primarily on the degree to which the consultant respects differences in perspective, is open and genuine, and is willing to learn.

Some of the issues that seem relevant to successful international consulting (Lippitt & Hoopes, 1978) have been identified, and these are summarized in this chapter.

---

[22]This chapter is a working paper that was developed by Gordon Lippitt. He is the sole author of this contribution.

CULTURAL ISSUES

Viewing Culture As a Means of Understanding People

It is important for the consultant to observe what is happening in the surrounding human environment, to look for value differences, and to appreciate their importance. A concern for culture may be as important as a concern with the client's needs. An understanding of culture enables a consultant to empathize and to communicate with clarity and understanding. In many countries, for example, religion plays a critical role in the way people live; and the working week is unlike that in the United States due to the religious holidays that they observe.

Collecting Valid Data

Joining forces with an internal consultant or a skilled member of the host culture can be an excellent way for a consultant to collect data. One's data gathering must take into account cultural attitudes and behaviors. An American or British consultant, in particular, must resist the temptation to collect data only from English-speaking nationals. These people almost always have been educated in Canada, England, or the United States; and they have perceptions of the country in which they now live that are not necessarily the same as those of natives who never have been exposed to an English-speaking culture.

Identifying Discrete Cultural Elements

Information about the particulars of the client's culture can be valuable. It is advisable, therefore, for the consultant to develop a plan to collect and analyze such data well in advance of an intervention so as to extract their significance and potential applications. If the client's country was once part of a colonial power, the consultant should be aware that the use of certain training materials or the selection of a consultant may be a sensitive issue.

Creating an Atmosphere
of Cross-Cultural Inquiry

In consultation it is helpful to foster an attitude of personal neutrality and objective inquiry (Harris & Moran, 1981). Of course, this calls for rigid suspension of judgment on the part of both consultant and client until all the issues have been thoroughly explored and mutually recognized. It is good to start from a searching posture and to encourage a straightforward discussion of consultant and client biases that might inhibit a problem-solving process.

The consultant also should admit limited understanding of the country's political and cultural history. Otherwise, the client or his or her representatives may come to believe that the consultant knows more than is actually the case.

Overcoming Language As a Difficulty

Some clients may resent a consultant's inability to speak the native language. The consultant need not be fluent in that language, but an effort to use some of the common words and phrases is almost always appreciated.

Although an inability to speak the client's language can be detrimental to a consultative effort, other factors can mitigate such a deficiency, such as the ability to relate effectively through an approach that is honest, sincere, and caring and the capacity for making appropriate responses to a real and strong need for assistance. It may be that the need for language competence is in direct proportion to the duration of the consultation. In the long run, there may even be an advantage in not knowing the language well if this lack of knowledge serves to reduce the perceived threat that all clients experience with verbally proficient consultants.

Adapting a Model to a Client's
Specific Situation

A personnel system that works well in Chicago, for instance, may be entirely inappropriate for a client in another country because of cultural differences; similarly, a presentation of how an intervention should work in Chicago may be totally inappropriate in another country. The consultant's values regarding both theory and practice will almost surely be in conflict in some way with those of the client. Therefore, it is important for the consultant to be flexible in offering alternatives for implementation.

Negotiating Role Expectations

The tendency of clients in certain cultures to adopt a dependent role needs to be addressed so that the relationship between consultant and client becomes interdependent. Problem-solving situations must be clearly described, and the roles of those involved must be clarified. The assumption of roles in the relationship should be voluntary; the consultant may not be aware of culture-based resistance to assuming certain kinds of roles. Care should be taken to see that both the consultant's and the client's needs with regard to roles are adequately met.

Acknowledging Client Attitudes Toward Past, Present, and Future

Although management consulting is implicitly oriented toward the future, clients in some countries may culturally value the past or the status quo more than they appreciate what might be accomplished in the future. In fact, change may be viewed as a negative phenomenon. Because the consultant undoubtedly believes that he or she has been brought into the picture to introduce change, or at least to propose its serious consideration, this conflict cannot be avoided entirely; it can, however, be ameliorated. The consultant should find effective ways of demonstrating the implications of the changing world to which everyone must respond. It is important for the consultant to communicate the fact that his or her goal is an improved quality of life that is consistent with the time parameters of the client's culture.

Legitimizing Cultural Differences

It is helpful for the consultant to discover the living patterns that are unique to the client's culture and to respect these patterns. Whether these traditions include observing a rigid time schedule for a tea break or showing respect for age or position, it is advantageous to recognize and honor them.

In order to deliver services effectively, the consultant must establish a strong relationship with the client based on trust, openness, and interdependence. The establishment of such a relationship is easier for the consultant who understands any relevant value differences and is able to adapt his or her input to the cultural perspective of the client. Consequently, the consultant should explore, as a part of the consultation process, all of the prevalent assumptions, styles, behavior patterns, modes of communication, and ways of thinking that characterize the client's culture.

Understanding Oneself

In order to help the client avoid the culture shock that can result from confronting the new and different, the consultant must be sensitive to the way in which he or she is perceived by the client. To cultivate this sensitivity, the consultant needs to develop self-understanding and a willingness to accept feedback about his or her behavior. These suggestions may be helpful:

- Develop a performance-based competency model of consultation in order to keep on track; and
- Always be willing to collaborate with others for personal and professional development.

CONSULTANT ISSUES

Maintaining Dependence of Client

A situation in which the consultant tries to keep the client dependent on him or her is undesirable. The consultant should avoid a posture that perpetuates inequality. Eventually such a stance leads the client to feel inadequate and to become defensive, passive, and/or resistant to change. As a matter of fact, in some cultures, a consultant's attempt to appear superior may be seen as projection of a past history of domination by outsiders.

Acknowledging the Positive Worth of Differences

Failure to acknowledge differences and their positive worth may create an ever-widening gap between consultant and client, magnifying fear of the unknown, breeding apprehension, and inhibiting the development of a mutually supportive relationship. In contrast, admitting and probing these differences can lead to mutual understanding and the development of an effective consultant-client team.

However, the consultant is advised to determine whether conflict of any scope with a particular culture is consensus oriented, politically oriented, time-lapse oriented, or confrontation oriented. Once this determination has been made, the consultant can adapt accordingly.

Relying on an Internal Linking Agent

Paying undue attention to the concerns of a linking agent in a client organization can cause the consultant to lose objectivity or to develop a biased data base. Forming such a relationship reduces the consultant's responsiveness to other representatives of the client system.

Another important concern with regard to the issue of leaning too heavily on a linking agent is that the consulting contract itself might be jeopardized if that agent is replaced. In fact, the consultant would be well advised to make both formal and informal contacts in the client's country at several socioeconomic levels.

Presenting Oneself to the Client

The manner in which the consultant presents himself or herself with respect to credentials, behavior, dress, language use, and openness should be facilitating rather than distracting. This certainly includes being aware of language and behavior that may be offensive in the client's culture.

However, the consultant should be comfortable, natural, and sincere in dealing with the client; to be seen as artificial or as unduly trying to impress the client by adopting local customs can cause the consultant to lose credibility. The cardinal rule is to adapt to the culture without straining to adopt all of its external manifestations. For example, the consultant should not assume a native style of dress that he or she finds uncomfortable or personally inappropriate.

Asking for Feedback

Giving feedback may not be a normal, everyday practice in the client's culture; the skills for giving and receiving such data may not exist. Therefore, the consultant may have to build into the contract a recognition of the need for feedback and the training required to exercise it. Prematurely eliciting feedback may result in client evaluations and judgments that adversely affect the contractual relationship.

Isolating Oneself

Relating only to people of one's own culture while in a foreign country might seem less risky to the consultant; but in actuality such an attitude may have negative overtones, both professionally and personally. Proper behavior that creates a climate of interested involvement gives the consultant visibility and provides fewer opportunities for the natives to make erroneous assumptions. The consultant should be aware that in many cultures people expect a more personal type of relationship than is typical in North America.

Maintaining Information Flow

The consultant's awareness of the effects of his or her behavior on others and the consultant's ability to use alternative behaviors can be a powerful tool in promoting a flow of information. Maintaining unnecessary psychological distance or posturing as superior to the client can dramatically reduce the flow of information between client and consultant. If the consultant's approach is genuine and involves the client intellectually and emotionally, whatever information flows will have a better chance of being heard. It should be remembered that in many cultures, if not most, people want to provide a warm and satisfying experience for a respected consultant; in fact, they may feel that this achievement is more important than the consultant's contribution on their behalf.

Facilitating the Success of a Co-Consultant

The consultant should not expect a native co-consultant in a host country to be a model of cooperative behavior. It is more or less up to the non-native consultant to create and support a common comfort level and to lessen competition by using team-building methods and by exhibiting self-confidence. The consultant can exert a powerful, positive influence on a client by demonstrating willingness to be cooperative.

Clarifying Who the Client Really Is

The person fulfilling the role of internal linkage is not necessarily the client. It is vital to understand the difference between the sponsor of the consulting assignment and the true client. Within a given client system the consultant may find a variety of clients, not just one; and these multiple clients may have differing and even conflicting needs and expectations. Success often depends on the consultant's lucid concept of the actual client in each situation. In a different culture the relationships among those served and those who legitimize the services may be far more complex than that to which the consultant is accustomed.

Risking Action

There is always the possibility that an action plan implemented in a cross-cultural setting may not produce the results envisioned by the consultant, and the consultant's fear of failure in unfamiliar circumstances can be an immobilizing force. The client's fear of failure, however, can be even more critical. It is important, therefore, that the consultant help the client to understand and deal with the risks involved in the implementation stage.

In addition, the consultant must keep firmly in mind that not only the action itself but also the implications of the action must fit the national character. The cultural history of a country invariably conditions its people's approach to any kind of action taking as well as their ability to handle both the fear of failure and failure itself.

Assuming the Posture of a Student

When appropriate, the consultant should be willing and able to assume the role of student without feeling a loss of professional credibility. This does not mean that the consultant must behave as a supplicant or in a self-effacing manner; it does, however, mean that the consultant should openly and graciously seek to be taught, even if he or she is not apt to learn much.

Involving Inside Helpers

Successfully finding and training teammates in the host country usually facilitates the consulting process. Adequate compensation to cover the expense involved can be built into the consultation contract. If the abilities and services of these insiders are essential to the continuation of the change after the consultant is no longer available, such compensation can be perceived by the client as cost effective. However, the development of internal talent and ability can be difficult to manage and, unless carefully handled, may adversely affect the consultant's future relationships with members of the client system.

CLIENT ISSUES

Lack of Client Cooperation

Sometimes it may seem to the consultant that the client challenges him or her to solve problems without any help. This frustrating denial of freely given feedback frequently is not attributable to anything that the consultant has done or not done; instead, it may be a national characteristic. Such a situation calls for a great deal of patience on the part of the consultant, who should proceed exactly as though nothing out of the ordinary is happening, anticipating that a thaw will take place in time. However, if this barrier appears to be unbreachable, ways should be sought to withdraw gracefully.

Absence of Clearly Articulated Request for Help

The client's inability to articulate such a request may be related to apprehension about being evaluated and judged, or it may be no more than discomfiture associated with admitting a need for help. This psychological hurdle can be encountered as readily in the United States as in another country, but here it is more likely to be a personal rather than a cultural characteristic. Overcoming this hurdle is essential to a consulting effort; working with only a vague definition of needs, objectives, and goals can result in addressing problems that do not exist and ignoring real problems.

Polarization and Differences Within the Client System

The consultant should avoid entering into a selective advocacy role or establishing a linkage with one part of the client system to the real or perceived exclusion of others. Those with a different cultural background may feel a compulsion to confront the consultant's values, attitudes, and objectivity. The consultant must deal even-handedly with all of the various factions that may surface.

Formulation of an Equitable Consulting Contract

The contract should clearly state the client's objectives; and, if the consultant and the client have different native languages, the contract should be written in both. This process does much more than concentrate the client's attention; it also lays the foundation for a contract that is fair and workable.

SUMMARY AND CONCLUDING COMMENTS

The three areas of cultural issues, consultant issues, and client issues represent circumstances that enormously affect international consultations.

Although the review presented in this chapter is limited and selective, it may be helpful in improving professional practice in cross-cultural settings. In summary, the following recommendations are offered:

- Be aware of values that are inherent in the client's culture, and thus avoid inadvertently condescending or disruptive behaviors.
- Become familiar with the significant, unique characteristics of that culture, such as its history, geography, art, customs, contributions, religion, and holidays.
- Take considerable interest in what people in that culture do and feel.
- Be able to greet people in their native language, understand basic phrases, and express those phrases with comfort.
- Prior to the consulting engagement and during the engagement as necessary, ask the client to explain any cultural and technical pitfalls, expectations, and potential problems.
- Arrive in the country well in advance of the work engagement and spend some time becoming acquainted with the culture.
- Ask questions frankly; do not insinuate, overexplain, direct, give advice, or act the role of "expert."
- Avoid openly comparing the client's situation with a similar one until enough is known about the current context and culture.
- Continually ask the client for assistance and collaboration; demonstrate the worth of the client's full response by showing how that response makes it possible to apply the consultant's unique expertise in that culture.
- Approach situational diagnosis and intervention with culture-based, *systems* thinking, not with a personal mind-set (Lippitt & Lippitt, 1981).

It is my feeling that consultants working internationally should approach their assignments as learning experiences and opportunities. International consulting is needed, challenging, fun, and rewarding; but it requires extra effort.

REFERENCES

Harris, P.R. (1982). Cross-cultural consulting effectiveness. *Consultation, 1*(2), 4-10.

Harris, P.R., & Moran, R.T. (1981). *Managing cultural differences.* Houston, TX: Gulf.

Lippitt, G., and Hoopes, D. (1978). *Helping across cultures.* Bethesda, MD: International Consultants Foundation.

Lippitt, G., & Lippitt, R. (1981). *Systems thinking: A resource for organization diagnosis and intervention.* Bethesda, MD: International Consultants Foundation.

10

Skills, Competencies, and Professional Development

This chapter examines the skills, competencies, and educational preparation required of an effective consultant—internal or external. We present a spectrum of attributes general enough to be applied to any type of consultant and consultation process in any field of work or in any type of client situation. By no means is this an exhaustive study of qualities that a consultant should possess, nor is it a manual on how to become a consultant; instead, it presents our perspective on the subject based on our own experience, ideas, and feelings as well as research data from practitioners in the consulting field.

There have been so few attempts to classify the competencies of an effective consultant that this lack has been commented on by Vaill:[23]

> It is difficult to describe consultant skills and abilities, and at the present time it is quite impossible to say how to train persons to practice them. Yet the issue must be addressed if consulting practice is to be effective.

Consequently, Vaill has urged that:[24]

> The critical need now is to collect more data on what these skills and abilities look like. . .and to talk with practitioners in detail, and, where possible, observe them at work, to see if these abilities can be documented.

---

[23]From "Organization Development: Ten New Dimensions of Practice" (p. 203) by P.B. Vaill, in *Optimizing Human Resources* by G. Lippitt, L. This, & R. Bidwell (Eds.), 1971, Reading, Massachusetts: Addison-Wesley. Reprinted by permission of the author.

[24]P.B. Vaill, *Optimizing Human Resources,* p. 211. Reprinted by permission of the author.

One of the difficulties in developing a taxonomy of competencies and skills is the nature of the consultative process as a personal relationship between people who are trying to solve a problem. The degree to which a consultant is able to influence this relationship is affected by four factors:

1. The consultant's behavioral competence;
2. The consultant's communication of helpful concepts and ideas;
3. The client's acceptance of the consultant; and
4. The client's legitimization of the consultant's role.

No matter how competent or creative the consultant, the last two factors—the client's acceptance and the extent to which the client legitimizes the consultant's role—are essential both to the consultant's opportunity to contribute toward the problem-solving effort and to the actual contribution. In this context, the professional behavior of the consultant is of prime importance. In the search for competency, the following questions may be useful as criteria for evaluating the consultant (Lippitt, 1969):

1. *Does the Consultant Form Sound Interpersonal Relations with the Client?* A consulting relationship is based on trust developed by effective interpersonal relations. The consultant should allow time for exploring this relationship in sufficient depth so that both parties feel that confidence and trust are likely to develop. If the consultant asks for an immediate, long-range commitment, the client may express reluctance about moving too quickly into such a relationship.

2. *Does the Consultant's Behavior Build the Client's Independence Rather Than Dependence on the Consultant's Resources?* Responsible and ethical consultants do not make their clients dependent on them; they understand that clients must develop their own competencies and capabilities and must seek professional assistance only when needed.

3. *Does the Consultant Focus on the Problem?* The reality of consulting is such that there always will be people who feel threatened, upset, and unhappy about the results of any consultation. Consultants who want everyone to like them or to be happy at all times may be insecure. They may dodge key issues rather than confront clients with potentially unpopular corrective measures that may endanger their continued employment.

4. *Is the Consultant Nonjudgmental and Tolerant Toward Other Consultants and Resource Disciplines?* Derision of other consultants or disciplines is the behavior of an unprofessional consultant. An effective consultant knows his or her own limitations and sees the value of others' specialties.

5. *Does the Consultant Respect the Confidences of His or Her Clients?* Another sign of a professional consultant is the ability to maintain confidentiality concerning dealings with clients. Some consultants attempt to demonstrate expertise, experience, and profundity by discussing the clients they have served. They may point out ways in which they "straightened out" organizations or occasions on which things went from bad to worse because their advice was not taken. However, a professional does not violate the confidence of individuals or organizations.

6. *Is the Consultant Clear About Contractual Arrangements?* Frequently, unprofessional consultants are vague about their fees or the conditions under which they will provide their services. True professionals set ground rules for their work so that a client knows what kind of services will be performed and the rates of pay on an hourly, daily, or job basis.

7. *Does the Consultant Appropriately Achieve Influence in the Organization?* Another trait of the unprofessional consultant is circumventing the line or staff person who brought the consultant into the organization. Although this tactic may enhance the consultant's prestige, it creates dependency in the organization and does not develop the capabilities of those whom the consultant was hired to help. Such a consultant does not build the resources of the client.

8. *Does the Consultant Truthfully Represent the Skills He or She Possesses That Are Relevant to the Client's Problem?* One sure sign of a nonprofessional is purporting to be not only a financial genius, but also an expert behavioral scientist, knowledgeable in quantitative methods and all facets of management. Such a consultant implies that the client has only to tap the consultant's resources on a regular basis to have all the competence needed for running an organization effectively. However, many consultants who are experts in one field may not be competent in another. Clients should be wary of consultants who unreasonably imply extensive knowledge and experience; they may be venturing far beyond the limits of their actual skills and abilities.

9. *Does the Consultant Clearly Inform the Client Concerning the Consultant's Role and Contribution?* Often an unprofessional consultant will claim certain work results when he or she actually is not accomplishing these results at all. The client who makes such a discovery should remove the consultant from the premises as quickly as possible. The consultant should clarify his or her role, including the potentials and limitations inherent in such a clarification.

10. *Does the Consultant Express Willingness to Have His or Her Services Evaluated?* Another sign of nonprofessional or amateur consultants is an unwillingness to have their work reviewed or evaluated

by the client system. Clients should exercise caution with a consultant who is reluctant to receive feedback on performance.

11. *Does the Consultant Participate in a Professional Association, Discipline, or Educational Process to Maintain Competency?* Professional resource persons should have ways of continually upgrading their skills and knowledge. Continuing education in a discipline and membership in a professional association are key ways for a consultant to maintain competency and current knowledge.

These common-sense criteria are based on the experiences we have had in both providing and receiving consulting services. This list is not meant to be exhaustive, but it does indicate major areas in which consultants should develop competency.

CONSULTING COMPETENCIES

Any list of the professional capabilities of a consultant is extensive—something like a combination of the Boy Scouts' laws, requirements for admission to heaven, and the essential elements for securing tenure at an Ivy League college. Nevertheless, we used a questionnaire to obtain data from thirty-two consultants on their own estimation of important areas of expertise (Lippitt, 1976). We asked the following three questions:

1. What are the skills, knowledge, and attitudes that are essential, in your mind, for a person to be able to carry out consultant services, processes, and activities?

2. What do you feel are the educational preparation and learning experiences that would equip a person to be able to function as a mature and effective consultant? (In other words, how could he or she become the person you cited in Question 1?)

3. What criteria can consultants use to evaluate their own effectiveness as it relates to the impact and contributions of their consulting services?

The responses we obtained from the questionnaire were varied, but certain trends were evident. It was obvious that consulting requires a multifaceted group of competencies. As one respondent put it:

In order to carry out consulting services, processes, and activities effectively, a consultant needs a host of multifaceted skills, knowledge, and attitudes. Some of these attributes are acquired, experienced, and known to the specialist, but I suggest that there are also internal resources, not consciously known to the specialist, that surface from time to time, and are dependent on situational circumstances.

In my experience of trying to develop three different OD teams in recent years, I have not seen any two specialists develop with the same intensity or pattern. This might suggest that we do not have any concrete rules of order that can be draped as the "mold" for a consultant. Those successful specialists that have evolved under my observation (some unsuccessful ones too) always seem to have a special quality that makes them credible to the client system. This quality may be charisma, professional competence, a flair for the dramatic, a warm personality, or a combination of all of these.

Another respondent listed the following abilities that are equivalent to competencies of a consultant:

- Ability to diagnose a problem;
- Ability to make an analysis and to interpret the results for the client;
- Ability to communicate effectively with all types of client systems;
- Ability to help other people become comfortable with change;
- Ability to maintain and release human energy;
- Ability to deal with conflict and confrontation;
- Ability to develop objectives with the client;
- Ability to help other people learn how to learn;
- Ability to manage a development-and-growth effort;
- Ability to evaluate results;
- Ability to be proactive;
- Ability to be creative and innovative in working with the client; and
- Ability of the consultant to be self-renewing.

Another respondent suggested the following:

In my opinion, all the educational preparation and learning experience in the world would not compensate for certain necessary traits and skills of the consultant that do not necessarily come from education. These include:

- Flexibility;
- Innovative and creative ability;
- Ability to quickly and accurately adapt to unfamiliar situations and circumstances;
- Possession of inner motivation (a self-starter);
- Extreme perception and sensitivity toward others;
- Ability to deal successfully with ambiguity;
- Extreme honesty (ethics of the profession);
- Genuine desire to help others;
- Profound respect for self;

- Optimism and self-confidence;
- Sincerity; and
- Charisma.

With these traits or characteristics, individuals have a much greater chance for success in the field of consulting than they would without them.

Summary of Consultant Competencies Derived from Questionnaire

When we summarized the responses from the thirty-two consultants, the competencies of a consultant seemed to cluster in the following categories of knowledge, skills, and attitudes. This summary represents one step toward identifying competencies.

Knowledge

Here are the specifics in the *knowledge* category:

1. Thorough grounding in the behavioral sciences;
2. An equally thorough foundation in the administrative philosophies, policies, and practices of organizational systems and larger social systems;
3. Knowledge of educational and training methodologies, especially laboratory methods, problem-solving exercises, and role playing;
4. An understanding of the stages in the growth of individuals, groups, organizations, and communities and how social systems function at different stages;
5. Knowledge of how to design and facilitate a change process;
6. Knowledge and understanding of human personality, attitude formation, and change;
7. Knowledge of oneself: motivations, strengths, weaknesses, and biases; and
8. An understanding of the leading philosophical systems as a framework for thought and a foundation for value systems.

Skills

The following are the specifics in the *skills* category:

1. Communication skills: listening, observing, identifying, and reporting;
2. Teaching and persuasive skills: ability to effectively impart new ideas and insights and to design learning experiences that contribute to growth and change;
3. Counseling skills to help others reach meaningful decisions of their own accord;
4. Ability to form relationships based on trust and to work with a great variety of persons of different backgrounds and personalities; sensitivity to the feelings of others; ability to develop and share one's own charisma;
5. Ability to work with groups and teams in planning and implementing change; skill in using group-dynamics techniques and laboratory-training methods;
6. Ability to use a variety of intervention methods and the ability to determine which method is most appropriate at a given time;
7. Skill in designing surveys, interviewing, and using other data-collection methods;
8. Ability to diagnose problems with a client; to locate sources of help, power, and influence; to understand a client's values and culture; and to determine readiness for change;
9. Ability to be flexible in dealing with all types of situations; and
10. Skill in using problem-solving techniques and in assisting others in problem solving.

Attitudes

The following specific *attitudes* are important:

1. Attitude of a professional: competence, integrity, feeling of responsibility for helping clients cope with their problems;
2. Maturity: self-confidence; courage to stand by one's views; willingness to take necessary risks; ability to cope with rejection, hostility, and suspicion;

3. Open-mindedness, honesty, intelligence;
4. Possession of a humanistic value system: belief in the importance of the individual; belief in technology and efficiency as means and not ends; trust in people and the democratic process in economic activities.

Change-Agent Skills

Menzel (1975) developed a helpful list of skills entitled "A Taxonomy of Change-Agent Skills" (see Figure 11). Menzel related his taxonomy to four key roles and phases of planned change, and he listed some twenty-five skill areas in his model.

Menzel explains his list of skills as follows:[25]

Change-Agent Skill	Explanation
Educating	
Researcher	Familiar with the theoretical bases for change
Writer	Able to write clearly and persuasively
Designer	Can design educational workshops and events
Teacher	Successful in helping others to learn
Instructor	Teaching related more to "training" tasks
Trainer	Beyond traditional "training"; able to "laboratory train," using heuristic methods
Advocate	Holding out for a point of view or plan of action
Conference Leader	Able to lead, and teach others to lead, a participative meeting or conference
Life/Career Planner	Able to help clients plan careers

---

[25]From "A Taxonomy of Change Agent Skills" by R.K. Menzel, 1975, *The Journal of European Training*, *4*(5), pp. 290-291. Reprinted by permission of the publisher.

ROLES	CHANGE AGENT SKILL AREAS	UN-FREEZING		MOVEMENT			RE-FREEZING	
The Process of Planned Change: / PHASES OF PLANNED CHANGE		1. Awareness of Need for Change	2. Establish Change Relationship	3. Diagnosis of System Problems	4. Examine Options; Set Goals	5. Acceptance; Take Action	6. Generalization and Stabilization	7. Termination
EDUCATING	Researcher		X	X	XX			
	Writer	X		X	X			
	Designer		X	XX			X	
	Teacher		X	X		X		X
	Instructor					X	X	X
	Trainer			X		X	XX	X
	Advocate	XR			XR	XR	X	XR
	Conference Leader	X			X	XX	X	X
	Life/Career Planner				X	X		
DIAGNOSING	Action Researcher	X			XX	XX	X	X
	Writer			XX				
	Diagnoser	X		XX	X	X	X	X
	Instrument/Survey Designer			XX				
	Data Analyst	X		XX		X	X	X
	Evaluator			X	X	XX	XX	X
CONSULTING	Role Model	X	XX	X	X			XX
	Relater at all levels	X	XX	X	X	X	X	X
	Expert in Consulting Processes:							
	Survey Feedback	X		XX	XX	X	X	
	Process Observation	X		XX	X	X	X	
	Decision Making		X		X	XX		X
	Problem Solving	XX		XX	XX	X	X	
	Conflict Resolution	X		XX	XX	X	X	
	Conference Leadership	X	X		X	XX	X	X
	Confronter	XR			XR		XR	XR
	Intervenor				XX	XX	X	X
	Systems Analyst	X		XX	XX		X	
	Designer/Planner	X		X	X	XX	X	
	Adapter		X		X	XX	X	XX
LINKING	Resourcer Linker		X	X	XX	XX	X	XX
	Internal Resources	X	XX	XX	XX	XX	XX	XX
	External Resources							
	Special Services			X	X	XX		
	In "thin" areas	(wherever help is indicated or needed)						
	Experts/Theorists							
	for Action Research			X	X	X	X	
	Referrer	X				XX		XX

Code: X-Relevant   **XX**-Especially Relevant   **XR**-Relevant but Risky

From "A Taxonomy of Change Agent Skills" by R.K. Menzel, 1975, The Journal of European Training, 4(5), pp. 289-291. Reprinted by permission of the publisher.

Figure 11. A Taxonomy of Change-Agent Skills

Diagnosing

Action Researcher	Knows how to utilize research and survey data and systems theory to apply to present situation in the organization
Diagnoser	Ability to identify what needs to be analyzed, what data gathered, how to obtain and use them
Survey Designer	Can get needed data in simplest way
Evaluator	Uses evaluation as an on-going process

Consulting

Role Model	Can practice what he preaches; congruent
Relater	Uses interpersonal skills to maintain credibility with all levels of organization
Expert in Processes	Possesses expertise in change agent's tools of the trade. Examples listed in the matrix; although also interventions, each requires "skills which have to be learned"
Confronter	Able to face issues and people head-on
Systems Analyst	Can employ systems approach to change process
Intervenor	Can use his expanding repertoire of interventions appropriately and effectively
Designer/Planner	Can plan and design and execute interventions forcefully
Adapter	Applies his own experience and that of others in a creative and relevant way

Linking

Resourcer Linker	Skill in linking the best resourcers with the correctly identified need
Internal	Identifies, enlists, trains, and employs resourcers within the organization to effect change

External	Identifies appropriate external resourcers, facilitates their entry and effective functioning. Uses internal-external consultant relationship well

Special Tactics

Where internal CA lacks skills or credibility	Three examples of linking functions where CA skills are employed
Theorist-experts for action research	
Referrer	Able to assist client in employment of resourcers who do not require CA's involvement

In his definition of the four roles, Menzel identifies consulting as separate from education, diagnosing, and linking. As indicated in Chapter 4, we feel that those roles are *included* in the multiple functions of the consultant.

Qualities of a Consultant

It seems to us that the qualities needed by a consultant fall into two broad categories: (1) intellectual abilities and (2) personal and interpersonal attributes.

From an intellectual standpoint, the consultant needs what we call the ability to make a *dilemma analysis*. A client who engages an outside consultant is probably faced with a situation that appears unsolvable or at least puzzling and difficult. The consultant must recognize that a dilemma, whether real or not, does exist in the minds of those requesting help. The consultant's role is to discover the nature of the dilemma and to help determine what really is causing it.

To cope with dilemmas (either real or not), the consultant must have a special type of diagnostic skill; and, as we have already indicated, the consulting process itself creates additional dilemmas. It is only through skillful examination of the client situation that a consultant can see the relationships between or among various subsystems and the interdependent nature of individuals, groups, and the environmental setting of the consultation.

Insight, perception, and intuition are necessary in order to make multiple dilemma analyses. Insight and perception are vital because the problem and the solution of almost any dilemma are part of a very complex situation. The consultant's toughest task is to penetrate the complexity and isolate the major situational variables. Unless the important factors are sifted from the maze of detail and the causes are separated from the symptoms, accurate diagnosis is impossible.

In addition to diagnostic abilities, the consultant needs implementation skills. Obviously, a consultant must have some basic knowledge of the behavioral sciences and the theories and methods of the consulting discipline. But, more than these, the consultant needs imagination and experimental flexibility. In consultation, dissolving a dilemma is essentially a creative process. No real situation is going to fit perfectly the mold suggested by typical techniques or textbook methods. Diversity and unique circumstances almost always exist. Consultants must be imaginative enough to innovate adaptations and tailor their concepts to meet real demands. It is vital for consultants to be able to envision the impact or ultimate outcomes of the actions they propose or implement. But, like most things, their work is as much a process of experimental trial and error as it is a matter of a priori solutions. The courage to experiment and the flexibility to try as many approaches as needed to solve the problem are crucial to the practitioner's effectiveness.

The other major qualities of the consultant are what we call personal and interpersonal attributes. Above all, consultants must be professional in attitude and behavior. To be successful, the consultant must be as sincerely interested in helping the client as any good doctor is interested in helping the patient. If the practitioner is primarily concerned with making a large fee or displaying competence as an internal staff member, and is only secondarily interested in helping the client, then the client will soon recognize and deal with that practitioner accordingly. People in trouble are not fools; they can sense objectivity, honesty, and, above all, integrity. One of our consultant respondents put it as follows:

> Perhaps primary to the role of a consultant is interpersonal skill. There are, of course, many variegations of interpersonal competence. This is one skill that quickly identifies you with the client system. Usually it is the first skill tested and continues to be tested throughout the relationship with the client. . . . It involves creating conditions of psychological success, of being creative in arranging knowledge gained with the client, an ability to develop conceptual models to explain or relate certain situations, an ability to exude and gain trust, an ability to recognize and handle conflict, etc. These skills and knowledges are ever evolving in a consultant.

After surveying the thirty-two consultants, we noted that all the responses emphasized the importance of the consultant's self-insight. As one respondent stated:

> Above all, consultants must be able to come to grips with themselves. Whatever views one may have of the client system necessarily interface with one's own value system, perceptions, and attitudes. Thus, consultants must be able to associate or disassociate their own internal constraints from those activities of the client.

Stanley M. Herman, a well-known consultant, expressed this very well in the following poem:[26]

Freedom 1

No one grants you freedom
You are free if you are free

No one enthralls you
You enthrall yourself
And when you have
You may hand your tether
    to another
    to many others
    to all others, or
    to yourself

Perhaps the last is worst of all
For that slave master is hardest to see
And hardest to rebel against
But he is easiest to hate
    and to damage

I do not know how to tell you to be free
I wish I did
But I do know some signs of freedom
One is in doing what you want to do
    though someone tells you not to
Another is in doing what you want to do
    even though someone tells you to do it.

---

[26]From "Freedom 1" by S.M. Herman, 1974, in *The 1974 Annual Handbook for Group Facilitators* (p. 246) by J.W. Pfeiffer and J.E. Jones (Eds.), San Diego, California: University Associates. Reprinted by permission of the publisher.

A consultant who is entering a client system needs a strong tolerance for ambiguity. From our experience one's first acquaintance with a client can be marked by a certain amount of bewilderment. It takes time to figure out the situation; and during this time one is going to experience a certain amount of confusion, as we indicated in Chapter 2 when discussing the entry phase. The consultant must expect this to occur and not be worried by it.

Coupled with the consultant's tolerance for ambiguity must be patience and a high frustration threshold. Helping a client to find goals and solve problems is likely to be a long and confrontational experience. Quick results, full cooperation, and complete success are unlikely.

If people think they may be adversely affected, they usually will respond to attempts to change their relationships and behavior patterns with resistance or dependency, resentment or overenthusiasm, and obstructionism or rationalization. It is important for consultants to be mature and realistic enough to realize that many of their actions and hopes for change are going to be frustrated. Such maturity is necessary to avoid reacting with the defeatism and withdrawal that commonly accompany the frustration of a person's sincere efforts to help others.

The consultant who objectively concludes that he or she cannot help the client system should, of course, withdraw and, if possible, refer the client to some other source of professional help. This act also requires maturity.

In summary, we are suggesting that the consultant should have a stable personality, conceptual sophistication, good interpersonal skills, and a good sense of timing. Timing can be crucial. The best conceived and articulated plans for change can be destroyed if introduced at the wrong time. Timing is linked to a knowledge of the client, to the realities of the consulting situation, and to the kind of patience that overrides one's enthusiasm for wanting to try out a newly conceived alternative.

Obviously, consulting involves dealing with people more than with machines or mathematical solutions. Consultants must have good interpersonal skills. They must be able to communicate and deal with people in an atmosphere of tact, trust, politeness, friendliness, and stability. This is important because the impact of the practitioner's personality must be minimized enough to keep it from becoming another variable in the situation involved and contributing to the existing complexity. Beyond this, a consultant's success will depend on persuasiveness and tact in handling the interpersonal contact on which the change effort is based. Because such an array of skills and competencies is not easily achieved, each consultant should continue to evaluate his or her own skill and style. Havelock states:[27]

> Most of the tactics or functions discussed (as interventions) cannot simply be picked up casually from a manual. They are skills which have to be learned. A good tactic badly executed may be worse than no tactic at all.

EDUCATION AND DEVELOPMENT OF CONSULTANTS

In our practice during the past thirty years, we have been grappling with the question of how to train, educate, and develop consultants. Unfortunately, consultant training has been, in general, a haphazard process. Only within the last few years have workshops and courses for developing consultant skills appeared. In commenting on these consultant-training opportunities, we have pointed out the following:[28]

> In laboratories on consultation skills for professionals of all types, some of the problems most frequently focused on for practice include how to:
>
> - Stimulate a need for help;
> - Give a taste of what it might be like to work together;
> - Develop a contract of collaboration;
> - Involve the appropriate client group;
> - Be supportive of working through resistance;
> - Stimulate change objectives or images of potentiality;
> - Get feedback to guide a consultation;
> - Conceptualize criteria for making choices among alternative interventions.
>
> It is a heartening sign that more and more professional helpers are accepting the idea that they also need help in practicing the specific interpersonal skills of intervention and designing consultation situations.

---

[27]From *The Change Agent's Guide to Innovation in Education* (p. 153) by R.G. Havelock, 1973, Englewood Cliffs, New Jersey: Educational Technology Publications. Reprinted by permission of the publisher.

[28]From "On Finding, Using, and Being a Consultant" (p. 2) by R. Lippitt, November 1971, in *Social Science Education Consortium Newsletter,* Boulder, Colorado: Social Science Education Consortium, Inc. Reprinted by permission of the publisher.

Some of our questionnaire respondents suggested the acquisition of quite an array of formal education, as indicated by the following:

I think the key to the preparation of consultants is a mixed background of interdisciplinary education and experience. It seems almost mandatory that they should have university training in some discipline and preferably several disciplines. A wide variety of disciplines can serve as basic training: psychiatry, general psychology, social psychology, education, political science, sociology, anthropology, business administration, or other of the behavioral sciences. What is important is that the practitioner have a working knowledge of many of these disciplines. It would also be desirable for him to have some knowledge of the technical disciplines such as operations research, general systems theory, finance, cybernetics, etc. In other words, a rather broad educational background with as much mix as possible, balanced against enough in-depth training in certain fields to have a very solid academic foundation in at least a few fields. The whole purpose of the mixed interdiscipline approach is to give breadth and scope to the practitioner, rather than narrow specialization. The problems involved in consultation tend to be interdisciplinary in character and not narrow. Thus, broad knowledge and multiple skills are needed.

Another respondent emphasized both the formal and informal nature of the educational development of the consultant:

I have concluded that a careful and rather precise developmental plan of education, training, and experience is required for consultants. It is the rare individual who acquires all of the ingredients necessary by happenstance.

First, I would seek out those professionals (Argyris, Beckhard, Bennis, the Lippitt brothers, F. Mann, Shepard, Schmidt, Tannenbaum, etc.) who are actively conducting, teaching, or coaching formal seminars or programs in consulting skills, conflict resolution, group dynamics, etc. These references not only have the appropriate academic reputation, but also have practical consulting experience with organizations. Studying or working with such persons would be invaluable.

Second, I would engage in a self-designed "readings" program. This would include not only an updating of selected texts, articles, and research papers, but also contemporary journals, papers, and magazines.

Third, I would join the NTL OD Network, ASTD, ORI Network, or similar groups, and participate in discussions, review of presentations, and exchanging experiences and papers.

Fourth, I would try to critique or make an assessment of my own strengths, attitudes, weaknesses, etc., and formulate a plan to strengthen my skills and knowledge along the lines outlined above.

Fifth, I would work at it. This means to actually take on different consultant roles with clients or join with another consultant. There isn't anything quite so valuable as residential learning experiences to stimulate personal growth as an intervener.

Sixth, I would attend a variety of professional conferences, laboratory sessions and special programs like the NTL/Bethel OD Program, the UCLA Behavioral Development Program, ITORP, etc.

In summary then, there are formal possibilities in behavioral science with universities and professional organizations which can help in preparation, but perhaps personal commitment to learn stands above all.

One respondent (Naismith, 1971) developed an interesting matrix of informal and formal learning experiences as related to the needed skills, knowledge, and attitudes of consultants (see Figure 12).

We agree with one comment made by eleven of the thirty-two respondents to our questionnaire. They indicated that an effective consultant should have had experience as a line manager or leader with a group, organization, or community. Such experience gives depth, reality, and insight to one's role as a consultant in coping with real problems, group decisions, organizational realities, and/or community conflict. As one experienced consultant put it:[29]

Help is never really help unless and until it is perceived as "helpful" by the person on the receiving end—regardless of the good intention or reputation of the helper or consultant.

It does require considerable knowledge and skill, as well as a flexibility of response, to be a professional consultant. As Schmidt puts it:[30]

For there is a time to confront but also a time to reduce tension:

A time to use power but also a time to use persuasion.

A time to act but also a time to diagnose.

A time to accelerate change but also a time to slow it down. A time to intervene but also a time to refrain from intervening.

But whether we confront or collaborate, intervene or analyze, let it flow from understanding and courage and love and not from ignorance and cowardice and fear—for these cannot long survive on any frontier.

In his reference to a frontier, Schmidt is referring to the organizational frontier facing the postindustrial society. Such a frontier is going to require all the excellence that multiple-discipline consultants and leaders

---

[29]From *The Leader Looks at the Consultative Process* (p. 2) by R. Beckhard, 1971, Washington, DC: Leadership Resources, Inc. Reprinted by permission of the publisher.

[30]From *Organizational Frontiers and Human Values* (p. 4) by W.H. Schmidt, 1970, Belmont, California: Wadsworth Publishing Company, Inc. Reprinted by permission of the publisher.

CHARACTERISTICS OF THE OD PRACTITIONER	MEANS OF ACQUIRING NEEDED CHARACTERISTICS							
	FORMAL EDUCATION					INFORMAL LEARNING EXPERIENCES		
	Literature of Behavioral Science and Organizations	Tutorial Under Experienced Practitioner	Individual Therapy and Sensitivity Training	Training Labs	University Courses in OD	Experience: Exposure to Organizations	Discussion with Peers	Experimentation
SKILLS/ABILITY TO:								
1. Use scientific methodology	X				X			X
2. Deal with people and situations; take action		X	X	X		X		X
3. Teach; communicate	X	X	X	X		X		
4. Diagnose and sense organizational problems		X	X	X		X		
5. Cope with political realities	X					X		
6. Detect success/failure				X	X	X		X
KNOWLEDGE OF:								
1. Change theory	X	X				X		
2. Characteristics of organic systems	X					X	X	
3. Self				X	X			X
4. A plan, conceptual model, or framework	X					X	X	
5. Specific OD methods	X	X				X		
6. Research tools	X	X				X		X
7. Organizational environment	X					X	X	
ATTITUDES:								
1. Trust; openness				X	X		X	
2. Flexibility, adaptability, learning				X	X	X		X
3. Desire to help				X	X			
4. Honesty with self and others				X	X			

Figure 12. Educational Opportunities and Consulting Skills

can bring to bear on complex and unknown problems. The challenge to those of us who dare to help both ourselves and others to cope with this frontier is clearly expressed by Schmidt:[31]

> Those who would live creatively and usefully at the frontier need now and then to pause and ask themselves:
>
> Am I prepared to live with uncertainty—to move before all the facts are in (they never are) or arranged in clear patterns (they seldom are)?
>
> Am I willing to risk a failure from acting now on the basis of my best judgment rather than waiting for others to take the first chance?
>
> Can I stay open to new learning from every experience—my own and others?
>
> Can I continue, even in crisis, to remember the humanness of those whose lives I touch—whether they view things my way or not?

If there are consultants with these kinds of values, attitudes, and beliefs, they may yet reinstate a confidence in all consultants as fellow human beings whose help can provide mutual growth for both parties in a consulting relationship.

REFERENCES

Beckhard, R. (1971). *The leader looks at the consultative process* (rev. ed.). Falls Church, VA: Leadership Resources, Inc.

Havelock, R.G. (1973). *The change agent's guide to innovation in education.* Englewood Cliffs, NJ: Educational Technology Publications.

Herman, S.M. (1974). Freedom 1. In J.W. Pfeiffer & J.E. Jones (Eds.), *The 1974 annual handbook for group facilitators* (p. 246). San Diego, CA: University Associates.

Lippitt, G.L. (1969). *Organization renewal.* Englewood Cliffs, NJ: Prentice-Hall.

Lippitt, G.L. (1976). *A competency-based survey of consultant skills.* Unpublished study, George Washington University, Washington, DC.

Lippitt, R. (1971, November). On finding, using, and being a consultant. *Social Science Education Consortium Newsletter,* p. 2.

Menzel, R.K. (1975). A taxonomy of change agent skills. *Journal of European Training,* 4(5), 287-288.

---

[31]W.H. Schmidt, *Organizational Frontiers and Human Values,* 1970. Reprinted by permission of the publisher.

Naismith, D. (1971). Unpublished response to G. Lippitt, George Washington University, Washington, DC.

Schmidt, W.H. (Ed.). (1970). *Organizational frontiers and human values.* Belmont, CA: Wadsworth.

Vaill, P.B. (1971). Organization development: Ten new dimensions of practice. In G. Lippitt, L. This, & R. Bidwell (Eds.), *Optimizing human resources* (pp. 203-212). Reading, MA: Addison-Wesley.

11

⊶⊷

The Consultant As Change Facilitator

The consultant's role is to serve as an agent of purposeful or planned change. This challenge has become more compelling and the necessary professional skills more relevant in recent years because, as Toffler (1971) has commented, "There is nothing new about change for it has always been part of man's history. What characterizes our modern era, however, is the increasing intensity, complexity, and pace of change. What once took years to transpire, now takes place in weeks. And significantly more people are affected."[32]

During our thirty-five years of professional practice as consultants, we have attempted to study the process of individual, group, and organizational change and to devise interventions that would most effectively facilitate beneficial change. In this chapter we share six facilitative strategies that are helpful in all types of improvement or change efforts, and we also identify common pitfalls that can block successful efforts when using each of these strategies. The reader may think of these strategies as a check list of change-agent skills.

STRATEGY 1: INVOLVING THE WORK FORCE

Frequently the process of planning and deciding about change goes on at the top-management level of an organization, and those who are expected to cooperate in the implementation of the change decisions are

---

[32]From *Future Shock* by A. Toffler, 1971, New York: Bantam.

involved in only minor ways. One of the evidences of the development of participative management is the use of innovative ways to involve the work force in providing input and reacting to plans for change.

Some pitfalls associated with involving the work force are the following:

1. ***Providing No Opportunities to "Buy into" Plans for Change.*** When employees who will be affected by a change are not brought into the process of analyzing the need and the rationale for that change, successful implementation will be difficult, if not impossible.

2. ***Assuming a Reactive Rather Than Proactive Posture Toward Developing Change Goals.*** We have noted that most organizations that are trying to effect change begin with an analysis of "problems" and "present pain" rather than with an attitude of creating images of desired outcomes. It has been our observation that starting from an emphasis on problems results in low morale and a lack of energy to put much effort into the change.

3. ***Failing to Create Plans for a Trial Effort and Revisions.*** A change should not be implemented without first setting up *tentative* plans, testing those plans through a trial effort, and then revising the plans in accordance with the results.

4. ***Projecting a Limited Time Perspective.*** Most changes require a significant amount of time to plan and implement.

5. ***Failing to Include the Participation of Credible Leadership Figures.*** Either formal or informal leadership figures can be helpful in presenting the need for a contemplated change and in providing a flow of information about planning the change effort.

STRATEGY 2: DEALING WITH AMBIVALENCE ABOUT CHANGE

When people are confronted with change, they usually feel ambivalent; they may be anxious about the time and the risk involved, but they also may feel exhilarated by the challenge and excited by the potential payoff. If this ambivalence is not legitimized as normal and expected, there are likely to be periods of blocks and hesitation during the change effort. This means that management should use various means of communicating the legitimacy of ambivalence as well as techniques that allow for the use of resistance as a positive resource in working out a creative change process.

The common pitfalls in dealing with ambivalence are as follows:

1. ***Labeling Normal Reality Testing As "Resistance."*** Reality-testing comments such as the following are often erroneously labeled as negative resistance:

- "I wonder if this change will require that we give up some traditions and values that most of us feel are important?"
- "I already feel overloaded; this just sounds like more time pressure and additional demands."
- "Nobody asked us what we thought of these ideas or how they might be made to work."
- "What new gimmicks are we going to have to learn?"
- "What kind of help are they going to give us in making the shift?"
- "Are there really going to be any positive payoffs for our customers or for us?"
- "There ought to be some options about when and how we make this change."
- "I don't think they've thought it through. I can see some possible side effects that I bet they haven't thought of."

If reality-testing comments are met with defensiveness and a determination to change the attitudes of those who make such comments, the change effort will be hampered. The evidence is not only that comments like these are normal expressions of ambivalence, but also that they represent one of the best ways to identify possible pitfalls in the contemplated change. In fact, much of the best creativity for implementing change lies in the ideas and the experience of those who ask such questions.

2. ***Assuming That Everyone Should Be Ready to Start at the Same Time.*** Those who have leadership responsibility for change efforts frequently forget about individual differences in the organization with regard to risk taking. When change is mandated for everyone in the beginning, negative consequences are likely. We have learned from specialists in planned change that it usually takes about three "waves" of involvement to generate readiness throughout the organizational population. For example, in the first wave the members of one department or unit may try a new procedure or technology. Then other organizational members become ready and motivated to participate in the second wave when they see the success and rewards achieved by those who participated in the first. After the results of the second wave become visible to the remaining members, these members become ready for the third wave. Managing these waves of involvement is one of the strategic skills of any change agent.

STRATEGY 3: ASSEMBLING TASK FORCES FOR TEMPORARY PROBLEM SOLVING

One of the trends of modern society is that the problems to be solved within organizations are becoming more complex and, consequently, require the integration of several different sources of wisdom and experience to solve. Also, it is often the case that each new problem requires different people to be assembled for the purpose of determining a solution; in other words, the same problem solvers cannot effectively solve all problems. As a result, temporary problem-solving teams or task forces are beginning to be assembled and used by organizations. Of course, this approach requires that the leadership of the system involved have available data about who is good at what as well as established norms of readiness and reward for temporary problem-solving assignments.

Some of pitfalls that we have encountered in assembling task forces are as follows:

1. *Using Political Rather Than Resource Criteria in Creating Task Forces.* There is a tendency to ask who needs to be represented rather than what types of resources are needed for the task and who meets these resource criteria.

2. *Neglecting to Identify and Use Unused Competencies and Informal Leadership Skills.* What is required is the development of a resource inventory stating which people are good at what, what kind of experiences these people have had in other job situations, and what aspects of their current assignments can be temporarily relinquished so that they can work part-time on temporary problem-solving assignments. The most effective procedures include not only identification of those who would be available, but also strategies for selling the idea to their supervisors and presenting the challenge to the identified people in such a way that they have a sense of voluntary choice rather than mandated assignment.

3. *Assuming That the People Who Are Chosen to Work Together Are Ready and Able to Do So.* Typically the different people who are brought together to form a problem-solving team represent different disciplines, experiences, and personalities. Thus, it is crucial to provide them with consultation and training so that they can hold effective meetings and can be aware of the process issues they need to cope with in order to work effectively.

4. *Permitting Alienation to Develop Between the Temporary Problem Solvers and the Formal Leaders of the Organization.* It frequently happens that supervisors become irritated as a result of the unexpected and unclear use of their personnel for problem-solving purposes. Often these temporary assignments mean that supervisors must find other people to fill in for task-force recruits. This alienation can be prevented by involving supervisors in the planning of problem-solving efforts, explaining the potential importance of the task-force work, and inviting supervisors to attend sessions as consultants at appropriate times in the life of the task forces.

STRATEGY 4: ESTABLISHING STEPS TOWARD PROGRESS

One of the discouraging aspects of many change efforts is that the way we want things to be seems to be so far removed from the ways things are; therefore, the idea of being able to achieve a successful change seems like an impossible or improbable task. To overcome some of this feeling, it is important to help the client plan individual steps that represent progress toward the desired change goal.

We have observed that the pitfalls involved in establishing steps toward progress are the following:

1. *Establishing Steps That Are Too Big and Too Long Term.* What often happens is that the more idealistic or enthusiastic the leaders of the change, the more they tend to focus on large steps and distant goal images rather than on small accomplishments along the way. This focus tends to maintain a sense of unreality and doubt about the significance of current activities.

2. *Neglecting Documentation.* What is being accomplished must be clearly documented so that it can be used for review, for presentations to management, and for a sense of assurance that things are happening.

3. *Failing to Identify Early Warning Signals.* It is important to watch for early evidence that an effort may be going awry. When such signals are noted promptly, plans can be reviewed and revised before too much time and energy are wasted.

4. *Neglecting Celebrations and Rewards.* The consultant should ensure that the client establishes a process for celebrating and for rewarding those involved when each step is successfully accomplished. It is a

critical challenge to "sell" the client on the idea of celebrating and paying attention to interim rewards rather than concentrating solely on payoffs at the end of the total effort.

STRATEGY 5: SUPPORTING QUALITY ACTION

The tendency in change efforts to focus on *what* to do often clouds the parallel importance of focusing on *how* the action is taken. Frequently a design for action is developed, but procedures for ensuring that the action will be high quality (and, therefore, have a higher probability of success) are neglected. There is nothing more damaging to a change effort than actions that fail or that achieve a low level of success as compared with expectations.

Here are some of the pitfalls connected with supporting quality action:

1. *Neglecting Rehearsal Before Risk Taking.* There are many times during a change process when the participants are faced with such risk-taking activities as reporting on progress, making recommendations to management, and designing and leading meetings for problem-solving purposes. In all these situations, the consultant must help the risk takers rehearse their presentations or activities before they attempt the actual thing. The consultant's repertoire should include skills such as facilitating role plays, simulations, and the visualizing of consequences, all of which can be used successfully for rehearsal purposes.

2. *Failing to Plan Pilot Tests Before Involving a Larger Part of the System.* In most change projects it is possible to reduce the risk of failure by planning and implementing pilot tests in small parts of the system in order to work out any difficulties in the design and to demonstrate to others the feasibility of the proposed effort.

3. *Failing to Obtain Support for Task Forces.* Task forces need nurturing if they are to be productive in a change effort. The support may be in terms of providing them with help in conducting effective meetings, locating resource materials and people, planning and making presentations to management, and identifying and celebrating progress.

4. *Expecting and Pushing for Independence of Action Instead of Interdependence.* Many individuals and groups believe that the most successful way to do something is to do it on one's own without any help. However, the fact is that asking for help is a sign of strength rather than a sign of weakness, and knowing when and how to ask for help is one of the major skills involved in successful problem solving.

5. *Neglecting to Review the Process of Work.* One of the most successful ways to improve the quality of work is to use procedures for periodically reviewing how the work is being done and how it might be done better. Every consultant needs to be able to help a task force avoid the trap of focusing only on tasks and ignoring process.

STRATEGY 6: MAINTAINING CHANGE MOMENTUM AND ACHIEVING CHANGEABILITY

With some clients we find that we spend as much as half of our time and energy working on the prevention of "entropy" or loss of momentum, loss of commitment, and loss of leadership for maintaining what has been initiated as change effort. Another continuing concern is whether as consultants we have been able to help the internal members of the team acquire the skills and concepts needed to help the client system cope with the new confrontations that occur continually in the flow of organizational life. Developing the attitudes, skills, and resources of changeability in the client system is crucial if a consultant's efforts as change facilitator are to be internalized so that successive change efforts can be addressed. A consultant's abilities can perhaps be judged best by the degree to which he or she has left behind the values and skills necessary to continue in his or her absence.

Some of the pitfalls that we have observed in connection with this strategy are as follows:

1. *Failing to Create Procedures for Progress Review and Performance Feedback.* As we emphasized earlier, establishing criteria and procedures for identifying and celebrating progress is a crucial aspect of maintaining motivated effort. This is certainly true with regard to maintaining a continuing change momentum after the first phase of excitement in solving problems has passed. If the effort has involved developing plans for individual development, then procedures for performance feedback must also be established.

2. *Failing to Support Documentation and Evaluation Efforts.* Supporting and reporting the significant payoffs of continuing change efforts is one of the responsibilities of the consultant and the internal change leaders. Those who do the documenting need to have significant status in the change effort through their roles as reporters of achievement, drafters of annual reports, presenters at professional meetings, and so forth.

The same is true for those involved in developing and continuing the effort of evaluation. Often the team responsible for evaluation and documentation has low visibility; instead, its members should be regarded as among the most important participants in the change process.

3. *Failing to Connect with External Sources of Support.* In most planned change efforts, external sources of support are essential in maintaining excitement about what is happening. Those who participate in the process of change need to be able to obtain periodic feedback from sources outside the organization about the evidence of progress, the emergence of problems that should be dealt with, and external innovations that might be useful.

4. *Not Using External Resources as Needed.* In maintaining the momentum of change, it frequently happens that new problems arise and must be solved, new personnel must be trained, and top management must be called on to participate in the ongoing activities. Sometimes an external consultant has worked vigorously on developing the internal resource team and then discovers that this team is thought to have all the resources needed to address any problem that might emerge. The reality is that no such team can be expected to be capable of solving all problems totally on its own; the use of external resources when needed should be assumed.

5. *Failing to Make Plans for the Professional Development of Internal Change Agents.* The consultant should help the members of client teams to plan their own professional growth; ultimately, these members should be able to take the initiative for selling management on their needs for other kinds of learning opportunities outside the system. What frequently happens as a result of rewarding and significant change experiences is that the team members and the organizational leadership begin to regard the present level of skill and competence of the internal resources as adequate indefinitely.

USING AMBIVALENCE ABOUT CHANGE AS A RESOURCE

One of our frequent techniques for legitimizing ambivalence is to distribute copies of an "internal dialogue" sheet. This sheet has two columns; in one column each respondent jots down his or her inner expressions of questions and doubts about the change, and in the other column are listed all the positive feelings about the change and its potential benefits. The respondents share their comments in each column and then brainstorm what could be done to help respond to the questions and doubts as well as what could be done to support the positive feelings and realize the potential benefits. This process opens communication with the leadership and provides the open feedback needed to deal with questions, doubts, and blocks to participating in the change process.

The following is a brief summary of some of the other consultation interventions that we have found helpful in dealing with and learning from expressions of ambivalence:

1. *Listen, Consult, Clarify, Accept.* The consultant should listen objectively rather than defensively to the client participants' ideas and feelings and should ask for clarification as necessary. One important fact to keep in mind is that client comments are frequently based on the assumption that their particular concerns and doubts are true of the majority, when in fact they represent a small minority. One of the effective ways of helping in this situation is to collect data from all or most of the individuals on a confidential basis and then present as feedback an analysis of where people stand. In this way those who are in the minority can learn, without stress and losing face, that they actually are in the minority. Often the consultant's listening, probing posture reveals important areas of misinformation; the challenge then is how to present data that will correct the misinformation without being perceived as being defensive. When the client participants see that they are being listened to, they are more likely to be open to new data and different points of view about the proposed change.

2. *Conduct a Validity and Feasibility Demonstration.* Being able to comunicate that the proposed changes are based on objective research or a knowledge base of some type is often helpful, but probably the most helpful approach is to arrange demonstrations or to bring in resource people who have related experience. Of course, something may be seen as feasible without being seen as desirable, but presenting data on feasibility and validity is still an important responsibility.

3. *Involve, Revise, Enrich.* The earlier it is feasible to allow the members of the client group to participate in thinking about the need for change and the nature of a potential change, the better. Usually it is possible to provide optional opportunities for discussion and input about anticipated or potential changes or at least to provide first drafts of change plans for discussion and revision. Often it is also possible during the first phases of implementing a change to hold debriefing discussions to suggest improvements and revisions. One of the most involving procedures, and one of the most helpful in fostering a high-quality change effort, is to have the participants brainstorm ideas about effective implementation.

4. *Provide for Rehearsal and Practice.* Dealing with the issues of anxiety and risk concerning the competencies required by the change is another responsibility of any change agent. Role playing, simulations, and in-basket activities provide opportunities to discover what the change will be like and to rehearse ways of coping with new tasks and expectations. These rehearsal situations need to be set up as completely nonthreatening, and they should be presented as ways of learning how to be more successful and comfortable in the change effort. In all such techniques, supportive feedback and a chance to practice again are key elements.

5. *Support Action.* Rehearsal may decrease the sense of risk, but the real risks come at the time when action is being taken in an actual situation. At this point it is crucial to have a design for support that is close at hand. Such a design may consist of providing an opportunity for a telephone conversation or a debriefing session immediately after client participants try out a new activity, or it may be as simple as allowing clients to work with and be supported by peers. In most risk-taking situations of this type, it is important that the client participants work in pairs or in larger groups so that they can support one another and then review their experiences for ways to improve performance.

6. *Ensure That Progress Is Reviewed and Celebrated.* Because one of the sources of ambivalence is a sense of doubt about competence to do the job and the magnitude of the job to be accomplished, one significant way to help cope with ambivalence is to help the individual or the group involved devise a series of steps representing progress toward the change goal. These steps should include concrete specifications of the evidence that would indicate progress, ways to review the progress that is being made, and ways to celebrate achievements.

7. *Involve People in Further Planning.* Progress does not always happen. Sometimes feedback data indicate that unexpected difficulties must be faced. The consultant should emphasize to client participants that some further planning and improving will always need to be done as part of a change effort. The debriefing of evidence that activities are not proceeding as hoped or expected can be converted into an exciting challenge by having people brainstorm alternative possibilities and review their divisions of labor.

8. *Encourage Negotiation.* Sometimes the clarification of expectations and consequences regarding any anticipated change effort reveals genuine differences in values or in expected benefits and payoff. When this happens, negotiating these differences becomes important. Frequently a third-party helper may be needed in a negotiation process that explores

the balance of benefits and the balance of sacrifices and reviews potential payoff. The best outcome of this process may be that people agree to give the change effort a try, see what happens, and then review how they feel about it. In this type of negotiation process it is important that people understand that commitments and decisions are not irreversible and that the payoffs of the change effort will be reviewed at some specific time.

All of these approaches to the use of ambivalence as a resource for building a more creative change process are based on two assumptions. One is that anyone who will be affected by the implementation of a change should be involved in deciding about goals and means. The other assumption is that ambivalence is normal and that making it public and using it as part of a problem-solving process not only decreases the ambivalence itself, but also greatly enhances the probability of a successful and more intelligent change effort.

SUPPORTING THE USE OF TASK FORCES

It is our experience that after task forces have been established, it is crucial to provide a training session for the conveners on how to plan and lead effective meetings and support the work done by these groups. In addition, it is often helpful to have a periodic "clinic" session with the task-force leaders to share successes and to identify and help one another with problems. In Figure 13 we present a guide sheet that we have developed for use with task-force leaders and members to support a high-quality working process.

Your energy, creativity, and teamwork as a task force in planning, in acting, and in involving others are the heart of the change effort of which you are a part. That is why the success of your task force is so important.

Being productive and successful as a task force is a great challenge—and not an easy one. Assembling with your fellow task-force members to accomplish things that no one person can do is difficult and demanding, but it is also personally rewarding. Management's appreciation of your efforts will grow with time and with visible achievements.

Figure 13. A Guide Sheet for Task-Force Leaders and Members

The purpose of this guide sheet is to provide you with information about what you and your fellow members can do to create and maintain a vital, productive task force. Use it as an agenda for building your group, a tool for improving your productivity, and a check list of "dos and don'ts."

"Dos"

1. Narrow your "mission" down to a "doable" first goal. The next goals will follow after a solid first goal has been accomplished.

2. Be sure that someone is responsible for planning your meetings so that your time together will be used well.

3. Always be thinking about what additional people you need to add as resources for your action, and decide who should recruit those people and with what strategy of approach.

4. Always be thinking about division of labor in accomplishing your work: Who can best do what?

5. Keep giving yourselves deadlines, and help one another keep them.

6. Clarify your needs for help and the kinds of support you need, and ask your task-force leader to provide this help and support. Knowing what you need at any given point and asking for it is a sign of strength.

7. Consider whether two leaders rather than a single task-force leader might expedite your work. You might want to rotate leadership over time.

8. *Keep good records of your meetings, your decisions, your actions, your contacts, and your accomplishments.* Doing this helps to keep everyone informed, to orient new task-force members, and to clarify and celebrate progress as a basis for maintaining energy and support.

9. Project your calendar of meetings well ahead. Do not set dates from meeting to meeting.

10. Choose a place to meet that is comfortable and that provides good work space and facilities.

"Don'ts"

1. *Don't start by tackling too big a goal!* This is the most important "don't." Define some concrete, short-term goals or steps that will lead you in the direction of your larger purpose.

Figure 13 (continued). A Guide Sheet for Task-Force Leaders and Members

2. Don't try to do it all yourselves if your task force has only two or three active members. Put your energy and creativity into recruiting others to help, and then establish a division of labor to make things happen.

3. Don't assemble for a meeting without having a plan for that meeting and what you want to accomplish by the time it has ended.

4. Don't assume that important people will say "no" to your requests and, therefore, avoid approaching them. Just concentrate on the best strategy for obtaining their interest.

5. Don't assume that it is better to "do it all" by yourselves. One of the greatest strengths is asking for help at the right time from the right person.

Planning a Good Meeting

Two leaders usually can do a better job of planning meetings than one. If your task force has only one leader, that person should ask one or two members to work with him or her in planning meetings. *A good meeting cannot just happen!* It must be creatively thought out, and an agenda must be prepared. The items to cover at a presession to plan a meeting are as follows:

- What the best flow of the agenda might be;
- What people can do as they arrive and before everyone is present (what articles can be read, which issues can be thought about or discussed, and so forth);
- How to obtain reports of what has happened since the last meeting;
- How to start the discussion of each agenda item;
- Which items call for discussion, which ones are strictly for informational purposes, which need brainstorming but not decisions, and so forth;
- How much time might be required for each agenda item (presented to the task force as a working plan);
- Who will be asked to present each item; and
- Who will bring what needed supplies, arrange for coffee, and so forth.

After the Meeting

Either the same day or the next day, the task-force leader should hold a "debriefing review" of the meeting with the co-leader or the informal planning team. This review can be held over the phone if it is too difficult for these people to get together. This "post-mortem" should include the following items:

Figure 13 (continued). A Guide Sheet for Task-Force Leaders and Members

- How did the meeting go?
- How could we have improved it?
- What should we try next time to make it better?
- What kind of follow-up on commitments do we expect?

Although this list of items is short, it is important in terms of improving meetings over time.

Using These Ideas

The best chance of incorporating these ideas to make your task force stronger is to make sure that each member receives a copy of this guide sheet and that its contents are discussed at a task-force meeting. By agreeing to run the task force in accordance with these ideas and by adding to them, you and your fellow members will be building mutual expectations and the support that is necessary to turn those expectations into reality.

Some Characteristics of a Good Meeting

1. The furniture is arranged so that each person can see every other person.
2. There is a place at the front of the room to record ideas, preferably on newsprint so that the information can be saved. (Chalkboards have to be erased.)
3. An agenda is presented, added to, and agreed on.
4. There are time estimates of how long each agenda item should take.
5. Someone has agreed to record the members' ideas and the group's decisions and has committed to distributing copies of these records to everyone.
6. It is indicated in the meeting records who has agreed to do what before the next meeting, and the names are underlined in the records as a reminder.
7. Dates of future meetings are set well ahead (not just for the next meeting) so that all of those who are to attend can put these dates on their calendars.
8. At least once or twice during every meeting someone asks, "How are we doing on our way of working together today? Any ideas about how we can improve to be more productive?"
9. During discussions about issues or actions, the members consider whether anyone else needs to be involved and, if so, who.
10. Before adjourning the members summarize who will do what before the next meeting.

Figure 13 (continued). A Guide Sheet for Task-Force Leaders and Members

REFLECTIONS ON THIS CHAPTER

Gordon: No matter what kind of help you are giving to a client, it involves initiating and guiding a process of planned change and functioning effectively as a change agent.

Ron: From my experience the six strategies that we discussed are part of the challenge of almost any consulting effort.

Gordon: For me this framework of concepts and techniques to facilitate change complements the framework about the phases of consulting that we shared in Chapter 2.

Ron: What two ideas in this chapter do you feel are most important for successful consultation?

Gordon: I think I'd have to make it three: (1) rehearsing and practicing to ensure quality, (2) identifying and assembling the right people for task forces to work on particular problem-solving tasks, and (3) avoiding the negative labeling of ambivalence as "resistance" and using the dynamics of ambivalence as a resource in the change effort.

Ron: I agree with those, but I'm tempted to add a fourth: training task-force leaders before their first task-force meetings.

REFERENCE

Toffler, A. (1971). *Future Shock*. New York: Bantam.

12

◄══════►

Implications for the Future
of Consulting

TRENDS AND ISSUES
THAT WILL AFFECT CONSULTING

In this chapter we share a few of our observations about current trends and issues and their implications for the future of consulting and of those who practice it. It is our belief that all consultants need to become more future oriented about their profession and their roles in client systems. Although many trends and issues could be discussed, we believe that the following ones represent the priorities of the future.

Developing Images of Preferred Futures

One of the emerging functions of the OD consultant is to help client systems develop images of preferred futures as they prepare to do strategic planning. One step toward developing these images is to scan the environment and identify trends that will have a significant impact on an organization as it moves toward the future. In general, today's clients seem ready to search for clues about trends and about the cutting edges of changes and competition. Several areas serve as the focus of the search for trends: high technology (including communication networks), life style, the economy, politics, population, and distribution of resources. As clients progress in the environmental-scanning process, the consultant can help them move from identifying and summarizing specific trends to deriving the implications of those trends for their organizations.

Using Total Resources

Every organizational leader needs to perceive his or her system as a total human resource system, rather than as separate departments, units, or sections. Establishing a connection between trends uncovered in the scanning process and the implications of these trends for "total resource utilization" is an important challenge for today's executive. Closely connected with this challenge is that of integrating the potential and complexity of computer resources with those of human resources. One day recently we were working with the top executive of a major company. On his desk were three computers linked to different aspects of his company's functioning in Tokyo, Frankfort, and London. We asked him whether he experienced overload from trying to deal continually with such complexity. He replied, "Overload? I regard the multiple-message situation I face every day as the renaissance of intuition."

This dramatic statement also can be applied as a challenge to the consultant. Teamwork between the development specialists, the macrosystem specialists, and technology is critically required to respond to today's new trends and to those that will emerge tommorrow. General systems implementation will include all levels of the organization, so the OD consultant must understand general systems theory and its application. He or she will need skills to diagnose the effect of system change on employees and on the organization. In addition, the consultant will need to be able to mobilize task forces and ad hoc problem-solving efforts.

Centralizing Versus Decentralizing

In trying to help a large system cope with the challenges and puzzles of centralization versus decentralization, the consultant will need to assist the client organization in reviewing its mission, values, and functions and in establishing criteria for determining what to centralize and what to decentralize. There is a special challenge in encouraging the decentralization of decision-making processes and shared authority and in helping an organization develop a consensual vision about its identity and future.

We find it increasingly interesting and important to become involved in the deliberations and sensitivities of our clients regarding mergers, acquisitions, and divestitures. These are phenomena in which most OD consultants have not received training but that are increasingly a necessary part of a consultant's macrosystem orientation.

Managing Conflict

Conflict management and resolution have become an important factor in organizational life. The American Management Association sponsored a survey of managerial interests in conflict management. The respondents included 258 chief executive officers, vice presidents, and middle managers. The responses indicate that conflict is growing in importance and that the principle causes of conflict within organizations are perceived to be misunderstandings, personality clashes, value and goal differences, substandard performance, differences in methods, responsibility issues, lack of cooperation, authority issues, frustration and irritability, competition for limited resources, and noncompliance with rules and policies.

Despite these results, the respondents indicated that they devoted only 24 percent of their working time to conflict management. In some fields, such as hospital administration and city management, conflict resolution commands nearly 49 percent of the official time.

In the future a consultant's OD skills should include helping managers understand that conflict is a predictable social phenomenon that sometimes should be encouraged, tolerated, and channeled creatively into effective problem solving. The goal of organizational leadership should not be to eliminate conflict, but to use it appropriately. To achieve effective conflict management, managers should know the causes of conflicts, ways to diagnose the type of conflict involved, and methods to cope with differences. A key role of the OD consultant is to encourage the process of managing conflict and to find new ways to resolve disputes. In the future the OD consultant will help managers implement interpersonal approaches to keep communication open in the organization, to act as third-party facilitators when appropriate, and to develop such skills in others. There is an increasing recognition in today's organizations that third-party consultation is a crucial element of successful conflict resolutions.

Collaborating Among Organizations

Interorganizational collaboration is a recent trend that is on the rise. As limited resources and increased complexity confront the organizations of the future, sharing, collaboration, and support among organizations is becoming increasingly necessary. This development may be seen in such practices as the shared use of temporarily laid-off personnel and expensive equipment.

For example, one of us worked with an association representing seventeen cities that have pooled resources to maintain a staff of sixty-five key professionals and technicians, who, in turn, serve many of the needs of all of these cities. This design for collaboration required major changes in the attitudes of the citizenry as well as significant new learnings on the part of the professionals who are helping develop the competencies to support the required interorganizational communication, project development, and implementation. These professionals have been involved in training the city and organization leaders of all the cooperating cities in the skills, techniques, and risks of communicating effectively and developing the needed trust to carry out joint projects. Some of the most interesting developments as a result of this program include the merging of public and private funds and the extension of cooperation in such areas as productivity to such areas as quality education and special health care.

Changing Organizational Life

We have observed a movement toward the merging of line and staff functions in many important aspects of company operations. In an effort to reduce the number of management levels, many organizations are combining the role of manager with those of teacher, consultant, counselor, and trainer. We have been working with client organizations in which training and OD functions are frequently implemented by a network of line people who spend fifteen to twenty-five days per year at this task. Usually these people have been recruited for the task and trained by internal or external consultants. We also are finding that organizations are using task forces or product-development teams with greater frequency. In light of these developments, it has become important to have a cadre of line people trained as resources for leading and supporting these special groups. With this shift in practice, consultants will find that training trainers and providing continuing consultation and coaching to line people involved in staff functions will become a more significant aspect of their responsibilities.

Another change in organizational life is the increasing emphasis on identifying and supporting the use of all internal resources. Futurists tell us that technical, human, and sociotechnical problems have been becoming and will become more complex with each decade. This means that assembling the right people into groups to address specific issues will be progressively more important. Such groups will cut across the divisions of labor and will probably rely on computers as well as different units of the organization. As a result, OD professionals must become increasingly more competent with regard to developing human-resource inventories, identifying the types of resource materials and facilities needed for particular tasks, and helping managers develop the attitudes and skills necessary for matrix management.

Studies on group cohesiveness and morale indicate that high positive feelings within a work group do not necessarily result in high productivity. In fact, positive feelings may manifest themselves as collusion to work less hard or to demonstrate to management that the workers cannot be "manipulated." In order to respond to this kind of collusion in the future, managers will need the assistance of consultants in replacing their subordinates' traditional fear of authority with acceptance of goals and voluntary commitments, in encouraging people at all organizational levels to contribute to and "buy into" the mission statement, in fostering the development of people's problem-solving skills, and in developing resource-oriented rather than politically oriented criteria for forming task forces.

Increasing Pluralism

In almost all types of work and community systems, there is a trend toward pluralism, that is, a greater mix of ages, sexes, races, ethnic and social backgrounds, technical experience, and work experience. Multinational personnel are increasingly teamed in multinational corporations and international organizations. This trend can result in either more intense conflict or a complementary integration of values and skills to enrich productivity and the quality of work life.

In order to enhance organizational adjustment to increased pluralism, OD consultants must become more knowledgeable about differences in cultures, values, and perspectives of subgroups within a system. They also must be able to serve as third-party links in identifying and using complementary differences in assembling task forces, and they must be competent at handling issues of prejudice and insensitivity.

Integrating Human and Technological Resources

Managers in almost every work context are realizing that coordinating the human and technological resources required to accomplish organizational tasks can be an exciting challenge. Enthusiasm about becoming "computer competent" is being replaced by an awareness of and sensitivity to combining the right people with the right technology. Consultants must be able to respond appropriately to clients' needs to integrate these two crucial resources.

Balancing Individual and Total-System Needs

Perhaps the most important trend to which consultants must respond in the future is that of seeking a more workable and satisfying balance between the growth opportunities, health, and satisfaction of individuals on the one hand and the total organizational culture, structure, and productivity on the other. We find it increasingly important to encourage our clients to address this issue, which is one of particular concern to systems in which financial profit is not the bottom line, such as schools and hospitals. As economic and political pressures continue to necessitate "doing more with less," we believe that OD consultants will find it more and more crucial to start the consulting process with a thorough analysis of desired outcomes or the bottom line; only then can implications for changes be derived.

Widening Horizons

We have discovered that almost all of our clients fail to use environmental scanning as a basis for increasing alternatives in decision making. For example, we find that relatively few clients have ever tried to adopt the viewpoint of their markets or customers, even though many techniques such as simulations and role plays provide this opportunity. Helping clients to "widen their horizons" in this way will become a increasingly important function of consultants.

For example, recently we worked with a client with an international manufacturing base. During a workshop day focused on market planning and goal setting, the client participants assembled into four groups representing different competitors in different countries. In each group there was one member who had many years of experience in that particular competitive culture, and this person briefed his or her fellow members on the daily living and business situations that were characteristic of that culture. Subsequently, the groups engaged in role plays involving the different cultures. By midday the participants had gained some new insights that they could use in planning and decision making.

Another type of scanning that tends to be neglected is scanning competitive systems for significant innovations that might be useful to the client system. We have found that, with the exception of those who must maintain technological secrets, almost all people associated with any kind of innovation are eager to be questioned about what they do and how they do it. We have also found that sessions designed for the exchange of innovative information among professions are usually welcomed and appreciated by everyone concerned. Consequently, consultants should consider a proactive stance in the future with regard to fostering the spread of successful practices.

One of our most important discoveries in working with clients in this regard is that increasing the involvement of personnel in a system in a variety of scanning activities generates excitement and stimulates the input of significant ideas for organizing work and improving organizational practices. In one small organization in particular, it has become a matter of company pride to be part of a scanning group that meets periodically at lunch to put together findings and to convert them into implications for improvement.

Scanning Inward

Many organizations are the victims of narrow perspectives about themselves, their capabilities, their future potentials, and their resources. We have found that the practice of "scanning inward" can be fostered through the use of a human-resource inventory. Such an inventory should be computerized so that data regarding who is good at what can be retrieved whenever it is needed in order to establish task forces, product-development teams, and so forth. Typical inventory information should include the past experiences and training of all company members. In some organizations these inventories are called "skill banks." Collecting the necessary data cannot be done routinely with a paper-and-pencil questionnaire; people are generally not able to provide adequate data about themselves. Consequently, there must be a procedure for interviewing employees; and in the future consultants should be ready to help clients with such a procedure. In addition, consultants should be able to assist clients in accomplishing another important kind of inward scanning, that of developing detailed records of organizational failures, successes, celebrations, and heroes.

One strategy that is used almost exclusively in the public sector is to identify a series of temporary problem-solving challenges that need to be met by an organization and to offer these as opportunities for volunteer efforts. The reservoir of unused volunteer energy existing in every organization and community is virtually untapped. Consultants can provide valuable assistance in the future by helping clients make use of this untapped resource.

CONSULTANT GROWTH AND RENEWAL

As we worked together on this book, one of the important subjects that we sought to address was the consultant's ability to scan his or her own needs for growth and renewal. In connection with this concern, we considered the major differences among our colleagues with regard to focusing on quick reactions and solutions versus focusing on a deeper level of continuing development.

Although we agreed that some consultants want to keep up to date so that they can capitalize on fads and acquire new contracts, more typical are those who want to be as competent as possible and to have positive self-images as a result. Most want to discover the consulting roles that they find most challenging, and their goal is to learn as much as possible in order to challenge themselves continually. Even with the motivation to keep learning, however, it is not always easy to do so. The following techniques are those that we have found most useful in promoting our own learning during our careers:

- Listening actively to any colleague, client, or student who has an idea or experience to share;
- Regarding each client situation as new and, therefore, avoiding the automatic use of materials and designs simply because they worked previously with another client;
- Taking every opportunity to engage in co-consulting efforts and, consequently, learning from each other;
- Preparing speeches on new topics that require learning and organizing new information;

- Writing articles on topics that have been addressed in consulting sessions, preparing each draft as soon as a session has been concluded so that the information is fresh in one's mind;
- Continually exploring new concepts and models;
- Joining professional associations and thereby learning from colleagues;
- Organizing discussion groups that meet periodically to share ideas from reading and to discuss the implications of these ideas; and
- Finding one particular peer from whom one learns and with whom one shares ideas at an especially deep level, thus becoming clients of and consultants to each other.

Annotated Bibliography[33]

━━━

Albert, K.J. (1978). *How to be your own management consultant.* New York: McGraw-Hill.

> The application of consulting skills is covered, including conducting quantitative and qualitative analyses, planning for growth, and defining the scope of the problem.

Argyris, C. (1970). *Intervention theory and method.* Reading, MA: Addison-Wesley.

> This book evaluates the methods by which organizational intervention can be made effective. Part One discusses the goals of intervention, conditions under which decisions can be made, resources used to solve problems, implications of organizational deficiencies, and ways to deal with deficiencies. Part Two offers case illustrations of issues.

Bell, C.R., & Nadler, L. (1985). *Clients and consultants* (2nd ed.). Houston: Gulf.

> Articles on the dual aspects of the consulting relationship are examined in twenty-six chapters.

Bennis, W.G., Benne, K.D., & Chin, R. (Eds.). (1984). *The planning of change.* New York: Holt, Rinehart and Winston.

> This is a collection of readings on various aspects of planning change, particularly change in organizations.

Blake, R.R., & Mouton, J.S. (1984). *Consultation.* Reading, MA: Addison-Wesley.

> This book explores the field of consultation in terms of theory and practice, with emphasis on the various consultation approaches and their underlying dynamics in resolving problems.

───────────────────────────────

[33]Adapted from a bibliography written by G.L. Lippitt and R. Lippitt and distributed by Organizational Renewal, Inc.

Block, P. (1981). *Flawless consulting: A guide to getting your expertise used.* San Diego, CA: Learning Concepts.

Sample dialog and cases are used to describe consulting practice and behavior.

Dyer, W.G. (1982). *Contemporary issues in management and organizational development.* Reading, MA: Addison-Wesley.

This work includes aspects of planning and organizing, managerial and organizational relationships, and team building.

Dyer, W.G. (1976). *Insight to impact: Strategies for interpersonal and organizational change* (rev. ed.). Salt Lake City, UT: Brigham Street House.

Sections explore such subjects as the planning and implementation of organizational change, common organizational conditions that discourage or oppose change, ways to remove change barriers with effective change plans, and the nature of effective training as a means to constructive change.

Goodstein, L.D. (1978). *Consulting with human service systems.* Reading, MA: Addison-Wesley.

This book explores how various models of consulting theory apply to the special needs of nonprofit, human-service organizations.

Gollessich, J. (1982). *The profession and practice of consultation.* San Francisco: Jossey-Bass.

Various consulting models used in human-service systems are examined.

Gore, G.J., & Wright, R.G. (1979). *The academic consultant's connection.* Dubuque, IA: Kendall/Hunt.

Although directed toward academic readers, this is a useful collection of articles on why consultants are hired, cost/benefit analysis of engagements, defining a service line, client character awareness, and team consulting.

Greiner, L.E., & Metzger, R.O. (1983). *Consulting to management: Insights to building and managing a successful practice.* Englewood Cliffs, NJ: Prentice-Hall.

This book deals with marketing, creating proposals, contracts, and bringing about change.

Kelley, R.E. (1981). *Consulting: The complete guide to a profitable career.* New York: Charles Scribner's.

This work presents a businessperson's approach to consulting.

Kubr, M. (Ed.). (1983). *Management consulting: A guide to the profession* (2nd ed.). Washington, DC: International Labor Office.

This book offers information on international consulting, models, and organizations.

Lant, J.L. (1981). *The consultant's kit: Establishing and operating your successful consulting business.* Cambridge, MA: Jeffrey Lant Associates.

> The business aspects of operating as a consultant are examined in this popular volume.

Lippitt, G.L., Langseth, P., & Mossop, J. (1985). *Implementing organization change.* San Francisco: Jossey-Bass.

> A two-year consulting project that The World Bank called "The Strengthening Project" is described.

Schein, E.H. (1969). *Process consultation: Its role in organization development.* Reading, MA: Addison-Wesley.

> This book introduces and explains the theory and practice of process consultation by focusing on the moment-by-moment behavior of the consultant.

Steele, F. (1975). *Consulting for organizational change.* Amherst, MA: University of Massachusetts Press.

> This book is a readable, informative, and thought-provoking account of the less-publicized functions and techniques of the consultant. It emphasizes the learning phases of consultation for both the client and the consultant.

Please add the following name to your mailing list.

_____

_____

_____

_____ Zip _____

Primary Organizational Affiliation: [ ] fill in with one number from below

1. Education
2. Business & Industry
3. Religious Organization
4. Government Agency
5. Counseling

6. Mental Health
7. Community, Voluntary, and/or Service Organization
8. Health Care
9. Library
0. Consulting

Please add the following name to your mailing list.

_____

_____

_____

_____ Zip _____

Primary Organizational Affiliation: [ ] fill in with one number from below

1. Education
2. Business & Industry
3. Religious Organization
4. Government Agency
5. Counseling

6. Mental Health
7. Community, Voluntary, and/or Service Organization
8. Health Care
9. Library
0. Consulting

BUSINESS REPLY CARD

FIRST CLASS   PERMIT NO. 11201   SAN DIEGO, CA

POSTAGE WILL BE PAID BY ADDRESSEE

UNIVERSITY ASSOCIATES
Publishers and Consultants
8517 Production Avenue
San Diego, California 92121

BUSINESS REPLY CARD

FIRST CLASS   PERMIT NO. 11201   SAN DIEGO, CA

POSTAGE WILL BE PAID BY ADDRESSEE

UNIVERSITY ASSOCIATES
Publishers and Consultants
8517 Production Avenue
San Diego, California 92121